FUNDING INCLUSIVE EDUCATION

Funding Inclusive Education

The Economic Realities

ALAN J. MARSH

ASHGATE

Published by
Ashgate Publishing Limited
Gower House
Croft Road
Aldershot
Hants GU11 3HR
England

Ashgate Publishing Company
Suite 420
101 Cherry Street
Burlington, VT 05401-4405
USA

Ashgate website: http://www.ashgate.com

British Library Cataloguing in Publication Data
Marsh, Alan J.
   Funding inclusive education : the economic realities. -
   (Monitoring change in education)
   1. Special education - England - Finance 2. Special education
   - Wales - Finance 3. Inclusive education - England - Finance
   4. Inclusive education - Wales - Finance
   I. Title
   379.1'19'0942

Library of Congress Cataloging-in-Publication Data
Marsh, Alan J.
   Funding inclusive education : the economic realities / Alan J. Marsh
      p. cm. -- (Monitoring change in education)
   Includes bibliographical references and index.
   ISBN 0-7546-0896-4
     1. Inclusive education--Great Britain--Finance. 2. Special education--Great
Britain--Finance. 3. Children with disabilities--Education--Great Britain--Finance. I. Title.
II. Series.

   LC1203.G7M37 2003
   371.9'046'0941--dc21

                    2003040361

ISBN 0 7546 0896 4

Printed and bound by Athenaeum Press, Ltd.,
Gateshead, Tyne & Wear.

Contents

List of Tables

Preface

...whose eyes glazed over when the question of funding and finance was raised...[1]

This book is concerned with funding inclusive education for pupils with special educational needs but without statements and is based on my PhD thesis. The writing of the book has been conducted in the context of a continuing concern that the cost management of special educational needs (SEN) and its effectiveness is becoming increasingly difficult. This has manifested itself in a number of ways but a common experience is the inability on the part of Local Education Authorities (LEAs) to contain budgets within previously agreed totals. A central theme throughout the book will be the national and international concern about the escalating costs of providing for pupils with special educational needs (e.g. Audit Commission, 2002a; Special Education Expenditure Project, 2002).

The national concern over the growth in special educational needs expenditure has led many LEAs to direct resources towards budgetary control as well as towards the identification of individual pupil need. Coopers and Lybrand in 1996 used the term the 'SEN time bomb' to describe the escalating budgetary commitments of pupils with special educational needs.

Concerns about the management and inclusion of pupils with SEN have been voiced by the Audit Commission throughout the last decade and more specifically by a joint publication by the Audit Commission and OFSTED in 2002. The Audit Commission have undertaken value for money audits in nearly all LEAs during the 1990s and have highlighted deficiencies in the 'Provision for Pupils with Special Educational Needs' which related to:

- poor framework of policy and strategy

---

1 Quote from Mr Robin Squire, MP who gave evidence as the Parliamentary Under-Secretary of State for the Department of Education to the House of Commons Education Committee 'A Common Funding Formula for Grant-Maintained Schools', 2 March 1994.

- lack of clarity about the roles and responsibilities of LEAs and schools
- lack of monitoring and accountability
- poor targeting of resources
- poor management and administration of the assessment process.

In 2000/01 about one third of LEAs inspected by OFSTED had unsatisfactory strategies for the inclusion of pupils with special needs and arrangements for the allocation of SEN funding were often unclear and obscured the respective accountability of schools and LEAs (Audit Commission/OFSTED, 2002).

In relation to these deficiencies, and in particular to poor framework of policy and strategy, the Audit Commission felt that LEAs, in general, had not been clear about the purpose of their SEN funding. A central point throughout this book is that a funding formula can be viewed as a key instrument of policy.

Since the implementation of the 1988 Education Act and the introduction of Local Management of Schools, LEAs have been faced with strategic choices in four main areas (Coopers and Lybrand, 1996a). These are:

- resource definition
- resource allocation
- resource management
- resource monitoring and evaluation

Whilst there is a considerable overlap between the four areas, this book is mainly focussed on resource allocation for inclusive education by formula funding and its associated links with resource definition, resource management and resource monitoring and evaluation. The research reported in the book has been carried out against the backcloth of changing legislation in the field of special educational needs and Local Management of Schools. During the course the book various sets of guidance have been issued by the government about the implementation of Local Management of Schools e.g. Circular 7/88 (DES, 1988a); Circular 7/91 (DES, 1991) and Circular 2/94 (DFE, 1994b). Additionally the 1993, 1996 and 2001 Education Acts and Regulations have received royal assent together with the 1998 School Standards and Framework Act which set out the new Fair Funding arrangements. Essentially the 1993 Act built on the principles and practices first set out in the 1981 Education Act. It also required the Secretary of State to issue a Code of Practice on the Identification and Assessment of Special Educational Needs which came into effect on 1

September 1994. The 1993 Education Act has since been superseded by the 1996 Education Act and 2001 Special Educational Needs and Disability Act. A Green Paper on Special Educational Needs was published in October 1997 *Excellence for All Children* (DfEE, 1997a) with an associated Programme of Action (DfEE, 1998a) and a revised Code of Practice in November 2001 (DfES, 2001c).

Although resourcing special educational provision in the days before LMS was a comparatively simple matter (Fish and Evans (1995), it was not without its own problems e.g. House of Commons (1993) and the Audit Commission (1992a). Formula funding was proposed by Local Management of Schools as an alternative method of resource allocation to the three main systems described by Knight (1993a). These are:

- historic funding
- bidding
- officer discretion

Historic funding describes the case whereby the school receives in a particular year what it spent the previous year modified up or down by a few increments. If a formula is well designed then it can be more equitable than historic funding since it can take into account changing needs. Bidding represents the case whereby the school puts forward a proposal for funding based on known criteria, however this can be costly to administer. Prior to LMS, 'LEA officer discretion' was used to allocate extra staff to schools where they judge the needs to be greatest. The method of 'officer discretion' is not as equitable as formula funding as it can be opaque and open to the personal preferences of the adjudicating officer. However there is a still ongoing debate whether more 'complicated' procedures for distributing resources are actually more effective or not and indeed what the notion of effectiveness means in this context. Although a strong case can be put forward to support the use of formula funding over other methods of resource allocation, there is still the problem of accountability.

Almost all LEAs have considered methods for identifying and funding pupils with special educational needs but without statements within their LMS/Fair Funding formulae. Yet the LMS arrangements gave no mention to how schools should be made accountable for the money that they received from the LEA for pupils with special educational needs but without statements.

> It will be for the school to consider how best to deploy its overall resources to offer the necessary provision....(DES, 1989a, para. 12).

Many heads and governors are unclear about where their responsibility ends and the LEA's begins. The Fair Funding arrangements illustrate an attempt by the Government to 'sharpen the lines of accountability so that all partners can received their rightful share of congratulation and criticism' (DfEE, 1998b).

The principle of accountability is illustrative of Coopers and Lybrand's fourth strategic choice for LEAs i.e. resource monitoring and evaluation and also of Chapter Three *Standards and Accountability* from the White paper *Excellence in Schools* published in July 1997 (DfEE, 1997a). The concept of a framework of accountability has been further highlighted in the 2001 White Paper *School Achieving Success* (DfES, 2001e). Further discussion of this important issue will take place in the final chapter of the book.

Acknowledgements

I am very grateful to the many people who have assisted me along my long and winding journey in writing this book. In particular I should like to thank Professor Rosalind Levačić, Institute of Education, University of London and Dr Derrick Armstrong, University of Sheffield for their generous advice, support and encouragement and to Professor Pam Sammons, Institute of Education, University of London and Will Swann, Dean of Education and Language Studies, Open University for agreeing to be my external and internal examiners at my PhD viva examination. I should also like to thank the education officers and teachers in *Whiteshire* and *Mercia* for participating in the research. And most of all, I should like to thank my family in their capacity as my 'personal backup team', for their loyalty, patience and understanding, especially during those dark and mysterious days of DOS.

List of Abbreviations

AEN	Additional Educational Needs
AWPU	Age Weighted Pupil Unit
CoP	Code of Practice
CSIE	Centre for Studies on Inclusive Education
DES	Department of Education and Science
DFE	Department for Education
DfES	Department for Education and Skills
EMIE	Education Management Information Exchange
ILEA	Inner London Education Authority
ISB	Individual Schools Budget
LEA	Local Education Authority
LMS	Local Management of Schools
NCA	National Curriculum Assessments
NFER	National Foundation for Educational Research
NSSEN	Non-Statemented Special Educational Needs
OFSTED	Office for Standards in Education
SEN	Special Educational Needs
SSA	Standard Spending Assessment
TA	Teaching Assistant

Chapter 1

Introduction

Aims, Key Questions and Chapter Structure

The main aim of the book is to investigate the principles and practice for allocating additional resources by formula funding, to provide inclusive education for pupils with additional and special educational needs (AEN/SEN) but without statements within the context of Fair Funding and Local Management of Schools (LMS). There will also be two subsidiary aims. The first subsidiary aim is to investigate how the purposes underlying differential funding for special educational needs affect the rules for allocation embodied in a funding formula. The second subsidiary aim is to examine the funding relationship for non-statemented special educational needs and pupils with statements in an attempt to develop a coherent approach to resourcing throughout the continuum of SEN. Each of the subsidiary aims is addressed through more specific key questions (see Table 1.1).

The book is in two main parts. Firstly, in Chapters One to Four, a theoretical component provides the key questions, a thorough analysis of the conceptualisation of special educational needs, an examination of the principles for evaluating a funding formula and provides a critique of Fair Funding/LMS and its effects on special educational needs. Secondly, in Chapters Five and Six, there is an empirical component, which presents evidence from two national surveys and case studies from two LEAs.

In Chapter One the aims and key questions are formulated. Chapter Two discusses the conceptualisation of special educational needs and also examines the two main purposes for allocating additional funding for special educational needs i.e. effectiveness and equity. Chapter Three presents a set of criteria against which school funding formulae should be judged. Chapter Four attempts to draw out the historic association between special educational needs with provision and funding by consideration of the pertinent government circulars of guidance relating to both of these areas.

The empirical and technical component of the book will focus on the areas of resource definition, resource allocation and resource management. Chapter Five considers current practice for funding AEN/SEN within LEAs by exploring two national surveys.

Chapters Six examines the resource allocation issue of how the quantity of resources allocated for specific forms of special educational need is determined. Chapter Seven provides the summary and conclusions. It will draw on the findings to the key questions listed in Chapter One. Particular attention will be paid to Coopers and Lybrand's (1996a) fourth strategic policy area of resource monitoring and accountability.

Table 1.1   Summary Table to show Aims, Key Questions, Methods and Chapter Structure

Main aim: to investigate the principles and practice of allocating additional resources by formula funding, to provide inclusive education for pupils with additional and special educational needs (AEN/SEN) within the context of Local Management of Schools (LMS) and Fair Funding.

AIMS	KEY QUESTIONS	METHODS
First subsidiary aim : to investigate how the purposes underlying differential funding for additional or special educational needs affect the rules or principles for allocation embodied in a funding formula.	Q1 How does the conceptualisation of special educational needs impact upon inclusion policy within Local Education Authorities? (Chapter Two)	Evidence will be presented from the literature about how the conceptualisation of SEN can be viewed from two main policy discourses i.e. 'special needs pupil' and 'school and teacher effectiveness' discourses.
	Q2 What contradictions and tensions are apparent when the purposes of providing additional funding for special educational needs are examined? (Chapter Two)	Further evidence will be presented from the research literature about the main purposes and principles which should be considered in detail when constructing or designing an AEN/SEN formula for inclusive education.

AIMS	KEY QUESTIONS	METHODS
	or criteria should be considered when evaluating a funding formula and how do they relate to the purpose of the additional funding? (Chapter Three)	
Second subsidiary aim : to examine the funding relationship between pupils with additional and special educational needs but without statements and pupils with statements in an attempt to develop a coherent approach to resourcing inclusive education throughout the continuum of SEN.	Q4 What have been the historical arrangements for funding pupils with additional and special educational needs? (Chapter Four)	Reference will be made to the government circulars of guidance and other research evidence from the literature relating to the arrangements and provision for special educational needs.
	Q5 What is the current practice in LEAs with regard to resource definition, resource allocation and resource management? (Chapter Five)	Two national surveys will be scrutinized to consider current practice in LEAs for resourcing additional and special educational needs (AEN/SEN) and will look at the areas of resource definition and resource allocation.
	Q6 What is the relationship between additional and special educational needs and resource levels and how does this match professional views? (Chapter Six)	Case studies will be presented from two LEAs (*Whiteshire* and *Mercia,* 8 schools in total) to examine the different levels of additional teaching arrangements provided for AEN/SEN pupils with and without statements. The school's special educational needs
AIMS	KEY QUESTIONS Q7 Is it worthwhile	METHODS policy will be examined

AIMS	KEY QUESTIONS	METHODS
	Q7 Is it worthwhile for LEAs to differentiate financially between different levels of need? (Chapter Six)	policy will be examined in detail and views will be sought from relevant professionals on the proposed resources thought to be necessary to meet the needs of specified pupils.

Key Questions 1 to 3 (Chapters Two and Three) relate to the first subsidiary aim i.e. to investigate how the purposes underlying differential funding for additional or special educational needs affect the rules or principles for allocation embodied in a funding formula (see Table 1.1). The DfES guidance (DfES, 2001b) on the Distribution of Resources to Support Inclusion provides assistance with the distinction between the terms of additional educational needs and special educational needs.

> Schools are required to support the diverse learning needs of different groups of pupils. These include pupils with special educational needs as defined in section 312 of the 1996 Education Act and those with other additional needs for whom some form of additional or different educational provision is required. Where the term Additional Educational Needs (AEN) is used in this guidance it is taken to include all children and young people for whom some form of additional or exceptional educational provision is required. Children with severe or complex special educational needs are included within this wider group (para. 1.4.1).

Key Question 1. How does the conceptualisation of special educational needs impact upon inclusion policy within Local Education Authorities?

A fundamental issue of concern to this book is a full consideration of the concept, definition, identification and measurement of special educational needs. A review of the literature appears in Chapter Two. Particular attention is paid throughout the thesis to Galloway, Armstrong and Tomlinson's (1994) set of policy discourses, which provide a good basis for viewing the problem of how special educational needs should be conceptualised. Galloway et al. consider that the confusion over the term 'special educational needs' is not essentially one of identifying criteria, but rather of deciding when the term is appropriate. They describe three areas of policy discourse which have emerged about the causes and the solutions to the 'problem' of widespread low and/or under-achievement. This book will concentrate on two of these areas. Firstly, the 'special needs pupil' discourse which places emphasis on a careful assessment of the individual pupil to determine whether extra support is required in order to meet the needs of that child. This discourse concentrates on identifying the supposedly fixed characteristics of children with special needs and is predicated on the notion of help for the individual child.

Secondly, the 'school and teacher effectiveness' discourse which is based on research demonstrating the impact of schools on their pupils' progress and behaviour (e.g. Rutter et al., 1979; Mortimore et al., 1988; Smith and Tomlinson, 1989; Sammons, Hillman and Mortimore, 1995). This discourse has grown in response to the overemphasis of 'within-child' variables or the concentration on individuals' deficiencies observed in the special needs discourse. The 'school and teacher effectiveness' discourse sees special needs less as a social construct than as the product of the failure of various aspects of the educational system to respond to real differences between children. This discourse is concerned with the whole school context and uses research which demonstrates the impact of schools on their pupils' progress and behaviour. Although there are important differences between the 'special needs pupil' discourse and the 'school and teacher effectiveness' discourse, the contrast should not be over elaborated, as school effectiveness research does not ignore the powerful impact of pupil background factors such as socio-economic status of pupils. School effectiveness studies demonstrate the strength of the statistical links between such factors and prior attainment measures in value added studies and argue that it is because of these strong links that 'like with like' comparisons with schools (which explicitly control for intake differences) are more appropriate than raw league tables of test or exam results (see Fitz-Gibbon, 1996). The concept of differential school effectiveness is also important and is discussed in more detail by Sammons et al. (1993) and Sammons (1996). Differential school effects concern the existence of systematic differences in attainment between schools for different pupil groups (those with different levels of prior attainment or different background characteristics), once the *average* differences between these groups have been accounted for.

A third discourse is also described by Galloway et al. namely the 'school failure' discourse, which is essentially a political variant of the school and teacher effectiveness discourse and sees the problem as poor teaching and outdated ideology.

In this book I shall reflect on the role that the discourses have played in the policy and practice of formula funding for inclusive education. It became clear to me that the discourses also constitute a theoretical basis for attaining an objective (Fulcher, 1989 p.8). If the 'special needs pupil' discourse occurred in relation to formula funding for inclusion and special educational needs, there should be evidence of factors and assessment information relating to the individual pupil. On the other hand if formula funding and special educational needs were to proceed according to the 'school and teacher effectiveness' discourse, it would be expected to have a focus on curriculum delivery and on the teacher's work rather than with individual pupils.

Significantly, during the fieldwork for this book, a general election took place in May 1997 and the new government quickly published a White Paper *Excellence in Schools* (DfEE, 1997a) in July 1997. The White Paper was felt by Hattersley (1997) to be based on the assumption that 'bad schools' are the products of poor teachers, who too often accept low levels of achievement as the inevitable fate of children from working class homes. This comment by the former deputy leader of the Labour party, echoes Galloway, Armstrong and Tomlinson's (1994) view that the 1988 Education Act was also based on the 'school failure' discourse. The Green Paper on special educational needs *Excellence for all Children* (DfEE, 1997b) published 3 months later in October 1997, built on the Code of Practice (DfEE, 1994a) with its emphasis on the 'special needs pupil' policy discourse. The two governmental papers give a good illustration of the importance of Key Question 1. This issue of the conceptualisation of SEN is a constant and important thread throughout this book.

Key Question 1 considers the impact on the development of the concept and the scope of special educational needs by the 1944, 1981, 1988, 1993, 1996 and 2001 Education Acts. The discussion will encompass children's rights and the definition, identification and measurement of special educational needs. It will also consider the views of educationalists who feel that a radical reconceptualisation of the state of provision for special needs is necessary (e.g. Dyson and Gains, 1993).

Throughout this book there is a complex interplay of tensions. A technical perspective of formula construction has to be balanced against a thorough analysis of the issues and consequences of following such an approach e.g. Barton, 1993. Such an analysis has been attempted in Chapter Two. Additionally the research reported in this book demonstrates that LEAs are moving towards more needs driven formulae to match provision and resources with identified needs (see Chapter Five). However this approach carries the danger of labelling or classifying learners in a way that places the emphasis on a 'child deficit' model of SEN without due regard to the contextual variables.

The outcome of following an approach resulting from the 'special needs' discourse is that there may be a reinforcement of disempowerment for both children with special educational needs and their parents. Armstrong (1995) has argued that although the 1981 and 1993 Education Acts have emphasised the need for parents to work together with professionals in the assessment of children's special educational needs, the essential concept is one of power rather than partnership.

> For children and their parents the outcome of partnership may, in practice amount to disempowerment by consensus. In these circumstances, the most effective partnership may be that which is forged through the strength of collective action against the structures of the state and against the imposition of needs by the state (Armstrong, 1995 p. 150).

The final Chapter of the book will revisit Key Question 1 with particular respect to the case study LEA of *Whiteshire.*

Key Question 2. What contradictions and tensions are apparent when the purposes of providing additional funding for special educational needs are examined?

Key Question 2 examines the tensions and contradictions pertaining to the purpose of providing additional resources (Chapter Two). Previous studies of funding arrangements for AEN/SEN have noted that in many cases the distinction between special educational needs and social disadvantage is blurred, in other words the purpose of the additional resources has not been defined. This point is crucial in policy formulation as it will determine future decisions about resource allocation. It will be proposed that there are two main purposes of providing additional resources for inclusive practice i.e. effectiveness and equity. A review of the literature provides a theoretical analysis of these two main purposes.

Key Question 3. What principles or criteria should be considered when evaluating a funding formula and how do they relate to the purpose of the additional funding?

There are a range of objectives or principles which provide criteria against which different methods of allocating resources for special educational formulae should be judged. The range of principles which LEAs need to address when determining their method of allocating resources for special educational needs, include operational simplicity, stability of funding, effectiveness, equity, efficiency, cost containment and accountability. It will be argued that the purpose of AEN/SEN funding will determine which principles should be chosen.

Key Questions 4 to 7 (Chapters Four to Six) relate to the second subsidiary aim i.e. to examine the funding relationship between non-statemented special educational needs and pupils with statements in an attempt to develop a coherent approach to resourcing throughout the continuum of SEN (see Table 1.1).

Key Question 4. What have been the historical arrangements for funding pupils with special educational needs?

An essential component of the research process is to explore the relationship for non-statemented SEN and pupils with statements in terms of previous historical funding arrangements. This funding issue is considered by desktop research and by reference to the pertinent government circulars of guidance (see Chapter Four). The relationship between needs and resources is illustrated firstly in Circular 4/73 (DES, 1973) which provided guidance for LEAs on staffing in special schools and classes, using categories of handicap and maximum class sizes. This guidance was updated by Circular 11/90 (DES, 1990) which proposed the concept of resource bands. Chapter Four also provides a discussion about the advantages and disadvantages of incorporating resource bands within a AEN/SEN formula.

Key Question 5. What is the current practice in LEAs with regard to resource definition, resource allocation and resource management?

Before embarking on the technical and empirical component of the research, I felt it was important to be aware of the current practice in LEAs in relation to the management of SEN. To this end, two surveys were conducted both of which have been made available nationally (reported in Chapter Five). Both surveys (Marsh, 1997a, 2002), have been published by Education Management Information Exchange (EMIE) and provide an analysis of current practice in LEAs for resourcing additional and special educational needs (AEN/SEN) in 1996/97 and in 2001/02.

Key Question 6. What is the relationship between special educational needs and resource levels and how does this match professional views?

Key Question 7. Is it worthwhile for LEAs to differentiate financially between different levels of need?

Key Questions 6 and 7 (Chapter Six) relate to needs and resource issues and examples are drawn from two case study LEAs *Whiteshire* and *Mercia*. Key Question 4 has already considered the government's guidelines referring to the relationship between special educational needs and resource levels (DES, 1990). These guidelines only refer to resource levels for pupils with statements of SEN and do not consider the wider definition, referred to in the Warnock Report (DES, 1978), of the '18 per cent of pupils' with SEN but without statements. Moreover Circular 11/90 suggested the use of resource bands but did not offer details of how they should be calculated, but stated that the resourcing model:

> ...derives from observations of classroom work seen to promote learning and care for various groups of pupils (para. 6).

One of the principles adopted by the Secondary SEN Working Group in *Whiteshire* referred to the distribution formula being sufficiently needs responsive to reflect the continuum of SEN. The Green Paper *Excellence for all Children* also makes this point (DfEE, 1997b, Appendix 2). Previous observations have noted that typically a resource based division is imposed upon the continuum of special needs, which has been termed the 'resource divide' (Dessent, 1987).

The EMIE surveys (Marsh, 1997a 2002), referred to in Key Question 5, show a trend in the AEN/SEN formulae towards financial differentiation between different levels of need. This trend is set against a previous finding by Lee (1992a) that most LEAs distribute their non-statemented SEN (NSSEN) resources as a standard unit cost. That is to say, each identified NSSEN pupil is allocated the same amount of money irrespective of the degree and the nature of the learning difficulty. To be equitable this practice would require all NSSEN pupils to have similar needs.

If LEAs are moving towards more refined methods of allocation, then it is important to examine the relationship between special educational needs and resource levels within the context of the school particularly at the interface of pupils which have a statement and those which do not have a statement. Key Question 6 develops the issue further and considers the views of relevant professionals from case studies carried out in two LEAs, on the proposed resources thought to be necessary to meet the needs of specified pupils. Key Question 7 considers the second form of equity, namely vertical equity i.e. whether financial differentiation is thought to be worthwhile within a formula.

It should also be remembered that there are other substantial funds available to help schools support and develop inclusive practice which supplement the Fair Funding/LMS arrangements. These sources of funding include the Standards Fund, the Schools Access Initiative and Education extra. The Standards Fund is a collection of specific grants paid to LEAs to achieve improvement in education standards set out in agreed targets, including those for inclusion. The SEN Standards Fund Grant 202 supports the creation of more inclusive education. In 2001-02 £82 million was available including LEA contributions. The Schools Access Initiative supports projects to help LEAs in England improve access to mainstream schools for pupils with disabilities including those in wheelchairs and/or with sensory impairments (with or without a statement of special educational needs). In 2001-02 £50 million was available to LEAs. Education Extra is an organisation funded from a number of sources including the DfES and various companies, Trusts and Foundations and is concerned with promoting out of school hours activities in schools. Individual grants are awarded from £100 to a top limit of £2,500 (Centre for Studies on Inclusive Education, 2001).

Chapter 2

The Conceptualisation of Special Educational Needs and the Purposes of Providing Additional Funding

This Chapter will be in two parts. First, it will provide an historical baseline for the origins and the development of the concept of special educational needs (SEN). The first Key Question will be addressed by this section i.e. how does the conceptualisation of special educational needs impact upon inclusion policy within Local Education Authorities? Second, the Chapter will examine the second Key Question i.e. what are the main purposes for providing additional funding for special educational needs? It will highlight the different funding implications of policies which seek to provide additional resources for specific pupils with SEN compared with those which seek to compensate for social disadvantage.

There can be serious limitations to approaching the development of education from the standpoint of legislative peaks, not the least of which is that legislation is at several removes from actual provision (Lodge and Blackstone, 1982). Nevertheless legislation is a kind of social stocktaking. By focussing on the preamble and provisions of the legislation a better understanding can be made of both the continuities and discontinuities of educational provision. The first half of this Chapter will examine four major pieces of legislation which have had a significant impact on the way in which special educational needs have been viewed. These are the 1944, 1981, 1988 and 1993 Education Acts.

The 1944 Education Act and the Origins of the Concept of Special Educational Needs

The history of special education in Great Britain is clearly and elegantly described in Chapter 2 of the Warnock report (DES, 1978). The opening paragraph is worth quoting in full:

Special education for the handicapped in Great Britain is of relatively recent origin. The very first schools for the blind and the deaf were founded in the life-time of Mozart; those for the physically handicapped and epileptic arrived with the motor-car; whilst special provision for delicate, maladjusted and speech impaired children is younger than living memory. Even so, the very early institutions were nothing like the schools we know today and were available only to the few. As with ordinary education, education for the handicapped began with individual and charitable enterprise. There followed in time the intervention of government, first to support the voluntary effort and make good deficiencies through state provision, and finally to create a national framework in which public and voluntary agencies could act in partnership to see that all children, whatever their disability, received a suitable education. The framework reached its present form only in this decade (i.e. the 1970s) (para.2.1).

The discussion leading up the 1944 Education Act and the implementation of the Act itself is of major importance when examining the history of special education. The 1944 Education Act led to the introduction of universal secondary education which developed along selective lines. Lodge and Blackstone (op.cit.) describe the 1944 Act as:

....both the central legislative pillar of contemporary education and the major expression of modern, formal commitment to social justice in education.

In June 1941 the Board of Education issued the Green Paper *Education After the War*. Although 'strictly confidential', the Warnock Report stated that it received a wide circulation. The statutory framework of special education at that time was set out in the 1921 Education Act which described school accommodation for blind and deaf children as being generally adequate, though much of it was old and ill-distributed. Less satisfactory was that for 'mentally defective' and 'delicate' children. It suggested that provision for most of these children should be made in ordinary schools. Therefore for the first time the notion was put forward that pupils with special needs should be taught alongside their peers. Two years after the 1941 Green Paper, the government issued its White Paper *Educational Reconstruction*. As in the Green Paper, handicapped children were included in a separate Chapter devoted to health and welfare, but this time they were dealt with in two sentences:

Provision for the blind, deaf and other handicapped children is now made under Part V of the Education Act 1921. This part of the Act will require substantial modification.

The 1944 Education Act can be regarded as a major effort by educationalists to move as many 'defective' children as possible out of the medical domain and place them firmly under an education aegis. The intention of the 1944 Education Act was to extend greatly the range of children's special needs for which local education authorities would be obliged to make special provision, either in special schools or in ordinary schools.

Detailed guidance of the provision to be made for eleven categories of handicap by local education authorities was issued by the Ministry of Education (1946). It provided estimates for each category of handicap of the number of children who might require special educational treatment, not necessarily in special schools. In sum these amounted to a range between 14 per cent and 17 per cent of the school population (DES, 1978, paragraph 2.49). This appears to be first mention of the figure 'the 18 per cent', which has been much quoted and generally acknowledged to have come directly from the Warnock Report itself. The intentions of this planning were not in the event fulfilled and special educational treatment came to acquire a much narrower connotation than the official guidance had indicated. Moreover its provision in ordinary schools failed to develop on the scale envisaged.

In the later 1960s and early 1970s things changed considerably. In particular, the completion of the reorganisation of all-age schools in the 1960s and the progressive ending of selection for secondary education which followed the issue of Circular 10/65 (DES, 1965) enabled mainstream primary and secondary schools to broaden their educational programmes and to take account of children's individual needs. Fish (1989) took the view that during the 1960s, there was an increasing dissatisfaction with the notion of ineducability, and with children being deprived of the right to education, the idea of education as any planned and systematic intervention to facilitate learning gained ground. New legislation was enacted. The 1970 Education (Handicapped Children) Act abolished the legal status of ineducability and made local education authorities responsible for educational provision for all children, whatever the nature or degree of their disabilities. The issue of rights and needs will be referred to again later in this Chapter.

In addition at the same time there were studies of compensatory education and the effect of early developmental influences. These provided a range of new evidence which influenced thinking about the causes of special educational need. These developments were reflected in the reports of the Plowden Committee (Central Advisory Council for Education, 1967) and the Newsom Committee (Ministry of Education, 1963), as well as providing one basis for the recommendations of the Warnock Committee. This area will be explored further in the second part of this Chapter.

The 1981 Education Act

The Warnock report (DES, 1978) and the subsequent 1981 Education Act represented the first attempt in the United Kingdom to take a synoptic view of the whole field of special education and to present a coherent philosophy and a blueprint for development for the rest of this century and beyond (Adams, 1986). The 1981 Education Act (which has since been superseded by the 1993 Education Act, the 1996 Education Act and the 2001 Special Educational Needs and Disability Act), introduced the system of a statutory multi-disciplinary assessment which could lead to the LEA issuing a statement of special educational needs.

Before the 1981 Education Act came into force on 1 April 1983, the provision of special educational services in England and Wales was formulated from the 1944 Education Act. Notwithstanding, it was still possible for Jones (1982) to identify 17 other 'Acts, Reports and documents relating to special education', many of which clearly represented quite major changes in direction for either special education as a whole or some aspect of the service.

The designation of 'disability of mind and body' in the 1944 Education Act indicated the weight given to 'within-child' factors as the cause of a need for special education. From this position, Goacher et al. (1988) describe the gradual, but continual movement towards a more interactive view of special needs, derived from a variety of sources, including studies of compensatory education, and environmental influences in general, as indicated in the Plowden and Newsom Reports. As a result, thinking about categories of handicap began to be replaced by the idea of a continuum of special educational needs. It became generally accepted that children could not be fitted neatly into handicap categories, and that special needs were often more complex than a single category would indicate. Furthermore the educational needs of a child could not usually be derived from a given category of handicap. Continuing with this view, an individual's special needs have increasingly come to be seen as the outcome of the interaction between factors within the child and within the environment (Wedell, 1981).

There was also evidence of the recognition of education as a compensatory resource in this interactive process. This was exemplified in the campaign by parents of severely mentally handicapped children, those deemed 'ineducable' under the 1944 Act, to force the government to provide education for their children. The parents' campaign culminated, in 1971 in the transfer for these 'ineducable' children from social services to education. It represented the acceptance of the principle that no child was ineducable.

The Warnock Committee therefore recommended that statutory categorisation of handicapped pupils should be abolished. The arguments against categorisation were listed in the Warnock report (paras. 3.21 to 3.25) and included:

- children can suffer from more than one disability (para. 3.23)
- labels can stigmatise children who are experiencing learning difficulties (para.3.23)
- categories create an assumed equivalence of educational need for all members of the category (para. 3.23)
- categorisation promotes too sharp a distinction between handicapped and non-handicapped (para. 3.24)
- focuses too much attention on the small group of ascertained pupils (para. 3.25).

The replacement of the within-child, deficit model by the interactive, ecological approach (Feiler and Thomas, 1988) carries with it the implication that for some children with learning difficulties, aspects of the school system itself may be the underlying problem. In other words there is a shift in emphasis from the 'special needs pupil' discourse to the 'school and teacher effectiveness' discourse.

In summary, the 1981 Education Act amended section 36 of the 1944 Education Act by imposing upon LEAs a basic educational duty to ensure that every child received full-time education which was not only 'suitable to his age, ability, and aptitude', but also 'to any special educational needs he may have'. Furthermore it broadened the concept of special educational needs to include any child whose learning difficulty called for special educational provision, and made it the duty of governors of ordinary schools to use their 'best endeavours' to provide appropriate in-house support. Moreover, because the Act provided for all children with special educational needs to be educated in ordinary schools (subject to certain conditions of efficiency), some commentators took the view that it foresaw the end of the arrangements whereby those who required special education, in the more restricted sense, attended segregated schools and units. In practice the evidence is limited that the inclusion of children with SEN has increased significantly over the years. Subsequent government action, reflected in Circulars 1/83 and 22/89 suggest that no serious change was envisaged, nor was there any process led by central government which might have achieved this end. The Green Paper (DfEE, 1997b) provides numerical evidence to support the notion that inclusion had not increased :

> Across the country as a whole, some 98,000 pupils are educated in maintained or non-maintained special schools, a number which has been virtually constant throughout the 1990s. (p45).

More recent statistics provided by the DfES (2002) demonstrate that between 1997 and 2002 the total number of pupils in maintained or non-maintained special schools, including those with and without statements, fell from 98,200 (1.2 per cent of the pupils on roll in all schools) to 94,500 (1.1 per cent). Norwich (2002) looked at the data for pupils aged 5 to 15 and found that the national percentage of pupils in special schools fell from 1.39 per cent in 1997 to 1.32 per cent in 2001.

The 1988 Education Reform Act

The next major piece of legislation to be considered is the 1988 Education Reform Act. A much fuller discussion of the impact of Local Management of Schools and Fair Funding will be covered in Chapter Four.

The original Education Reform Bill gave scant attention to the education of pupils with special educational needs, even though one of the notable aspects of its passage through Parliament was the concern expressed for children with special needs in both Houses and from all parties (Rowan, 1988). Many of the amendments were necessitated only by the discordance between the terms of the Bill and current thinking and practice relating to the education of children and young people with special educational needs (Wedell, 1988). The 1988 Act had as one of its main tenets the implementation of a 'quasi-market' whereby schools would compete directly with each other for pupils and school performance tables would be published to assist parents in their choice of school. Local Management of Schools, under which schools manage their own budgets, was another key policy of the 1988 Act. In addition a new type of school was introduced called a grant-maintained school. These schools were not controlled by the LEA and they have their own policies for the admission of pupils. In 1999 LEAs took over the funding of grant-maintained schools following the implementation of the 1998 School Standards and Framework Act.

The 1988 Education Reform Act introduced a further change through the implementation of the National Curriculum and Assessment. For the first time this placed an obligation on all schools including special schools to teach subjects such as science, technology and a foreign language to all pupils unless specifically disapplied. There is an overriding contradiction which has pervaded responses to the National Curriculum in special education as outlined by Swann (1992).

The National Curriculum was promoted as a curriculum for all children. Yet the contrary view was that it lacked the flexibility to be a true curriculum for all. The National Curriculum Council's own guidance: *A Curriculum for All* (National Curriculum Council, 1989) declared that:

> All pupils share the right to a broad and balanced curriculum, including the National Curriculum. The right extends to every registered pupil of compulsory school age attending a maintained or grant maintained school, whether or not she has a statement of special educational needs. This right is implicit in the 1988 Education Reform Act (p.1).

Bailey (1989) supports this positive view to the principle of access to the National Curriculum for pupils with special educational needs:

> The Education Reform Act should be viewed as an enrichment for all pupils with a widening of curriculum opportunities for pupils with SENs (p.78).

On the other hand some writers have strongly criticised the theory of learning which underpins the National Curriculum.

> How will young people, no matter what their attainment, ability or background, be able to derive a sense of equal value and worth in an education system which clearly articulates delineation according to attainment and the increasing compartmentalisation of fact and knowledge? A system based on discrimination – not equality and integration (Spalding and Florek, 1989).

All National Curriculum subjects are subdivided for assessment purposes into a small number of Attainment Targets set out in eight hierarchical 'levels' (DfE, 1995). English for example, has three Attainment Targets: speaking and listening, reading and writing. Each of these Attainment Targets have eight associated level descriptions. More recently there are now some further sub-divisions for levels 1 and 2 in English and Mathematics i.e. level 1C, 1B and 1A then level 2C, 2B and 2A. The level description for level 2A reading, for example, is

> Pupils read simple unfamiliar text accurately. Their independent reading shows they can read ahead and make use of expression and intonation to enhance meaning. In responding to stories, they identify and comment on the main

characters and how they relate to one another. They express opinions about events and actions and comment on some of the ways in which the text is written or presented.

A pupil is considered to be reading beyond level 2 when he or she has mastered the level 2 reading domain, that is, when the pupil's achievement in reading meets the criteria set out in the level 2A description above. This process of subdividing subjects into Attainment Targets, calibrated by level descriptions, allows all National Curriculum assessment to be referenced to a common 8-level scale with an additional description above level 8 to help teachers in differentiating exceptional performance. The DfES introduced performance criteria or P scales in 1998 to better enable the measurement of pupils' attainment below level 1 and at the early national curriculum levels. This guidance for effective target setting for pupils with special educational needs was revised in March 2001 (DfEE, 2001a).

As the central function of the National Curriculum 8-level scale is to monitor the progression of all pupils against an agreed set of national standards, it is important to ask if special and mainstream teachers share similar interpretations of standards associated with the lower levels of the 8-level scale. Wylie et al. (1995) set out to investigate whether there is evidence of differing perceptions of the standards between mainstream and special needs teachers such as would threaten the progression of pupils transferring from one type of schooling to the other. A previous investigation by the National Foundation for Educational Research/Bishop Grosseteste College (NFER/BGC) of the impact of National Curriculum assessment in special schools (School Examinations and Assessment Council, 1992) identified a degree of mismatch between the National Curriculum standards of mainstream and special educational needs teachers and found shortcomings in the quality of special needs in-service training.

> ...abundant evidence of concern on the part of teachers to conduct assessments fairly, that is, observing the same standards as would be applied to children without special needs (p.35).

Wylie et al.'s study involved an empirical comparison of the National Curriculum standards of three groups of teachers: 11 mainstream primary teachers, 10 special school teachers and nine teachers who taught in special units. All of the special needs teachers worked with children experiencing moderate learning difficulties. The study found no significant differences in the standards set by the three groups. Although the absence of teachers of children with severe learning difficulties may go some way in explaining the disparities between the two studies, the researchers felt that the result augers well for the progression of pupils experiencing moderate learning difficulties. They felt that meaningful progression to a transferring school would be better assured by the record of achievement which reports each pupil's level profile in each National Curriculum subject rather than a school report including results from a range of internal school examinations.

This optimistic view was not shared by Swann (1992) who warned of the dangers of replacing the previously flawed system of classification which had operated for many years before the 1981 Education Act with a classification system based on the levels of attainment. He claims that the organisation of the National Curriculum into levels of attainment involves the arbitrary classification of attainments to hierarchies of knowledge, understanding and skill, and the equally arbitrary assignment of levels to ages, leading to the arbitrary classification of children. Noss et al. (1989) and Brown (1989) also support this view that there are no linear hierarchies in children's learning of subject matter and development of understanding.

Despite these early criticisms about the use of National Curriculum Assessment (NCA) results, the debate moved on. The Code of Practice for special educational needs, implemented in 1995, made several references to the use of National Curriculum results when determining the threshold at which schools plan their additional action.

The full impact of the 1988 Education Reform Act upon the education of pupils with special educational needs is still being assessed even today. However Vincent et al. (1994) point out that SEN policy and provision varies very much from one local authority to another. These variations and their relationship with funding formulae have been explored by Evans et al. (2001) and by Marsh (2002).

LEAs were at different stages when the 1981 Education Act was introduced. Some used the Act as an opportunity to review their provision in its entirety, some made the minimum changes necessary to comply with the legislation (House of Commons Education Committee, 1993). However despite this variation, the recurrent concern about the 1988 Act is whether too much emphasis has been given to individual characteristics. This is clearly incompatible with the interactive nature of special needs as emphasised by the Warnock Report and provides evidence of the dominance of the 'special needs pupil' discourse.

The 1993 Education Act, the 1996 Education Act, the 2001 Special Educational Needs and Disability Act and the Code of Practice

The Warnock report and the 1981 Education Act have now been superseded by the 1993, the 1996 Education Act and the 2001 Special Educational Needs and Disability Act. In addition there has also been a Green Paper on special educational needs (DfEE, 1997b) which set out to improve standards for pupils with special educational needs and gave a clear commitment to promoting greater inclusion as well as the need to develop the role of special schools. A Programme of Action was published a year later (DfEE, 1998a) which undertook to review the statutory framework for inclusion in conjunction with the Disability Rights Task Force. The Task Force published their report in 1999 'From Exclusion to Inclusion' and recommended 'a strengthened right for parents of children with statements of special educational needs to a place in mainstream school. The statutory guidance was revised in 2001 (DfES, 2001d).

During 1992 the Department for Education issued a number of reports on special education which included two joint papers by the Audit Commission and HMI (1992a and 1992b). These various reports informed the provisions of the 1993 Education Act which required the Secretary of State to issue a Code of Practice under Section 157. A draft revised Code of Practice was issued in July 2000 and implemented in January 2002 (DfES, 2001c), six years after the original Code of Practice was implemented in August 1995. The purpose of the Code is to give practical guidance to LEAs, the governing bodies of all maintained schools and other agencies on the discharge of their functions in relation to children with special educational needs. The Code covers:

- a model of assessment including the role of SEN coordinators and support services. The revised Code replaces the five stage process with new stages of school action and school action plus
- the statutory assessment of SEN, including evidence required for assessment, conduct of assessments and time limits for making assessments and statements;
- the issuing of statements, including criteria for drawing up a statement, writing the statement, and naming the school;
- assessments and statements for children under five;
- the annual reviews of statements, including transition plans.

The original draft Code of Practice received mostly positive comments e.g. Wedell (1993). Upon publication of the final version (DfEE, 1994a), further favourable recognition was reported by Millward and Skidmore (1995), Bines and Loxley (1995), Lewis (1995) and Jowett et al. (1996). A detailed analysis of the Code's implementation in one LEA has been provided by Bines and Loxley (1995) who concluded that the Code can be seen as a mechanism for controlling and targeting resource allocation as well as a means of increasing accountability in relation to provision and partnership with parents. Ofsted (1997, 1999a) found that steady progress was being made in almost all primary and secondary schools in implementing the Code's main recommendations. However, that is not to say that the Code has been without its critics and clearly there are some significant issues which need to be addressed.

First, schools are likely to take a pragmatic approach to some of the more complex and demanding aspects of the Code, such as individual education plans and reviews which are likely to be developed and adapted in a number of ways. Jowett et al.'s (1996) research provides an insight into how the Code was being implemented. The research included a questionnaire survey sent to all LEAs in England and Wales and returned by 55 LEAs. Further issues created by the Code are that the ideal role of the SEN coordinator (SENCO) will be curtailed by limitations of time and other resources. As Bines (1995) has stated, the shift from curricular to managerial and administrative activity by SENCOs, which reflects a general move towards more managerialism in education and other public service reform, may also pose new problems in terms of the definition of the SENCO's role. Further commentators e.g. Vincent et al. (1995), take the view that the Code leaves the whole concept of statementing largely unexamined and intact, ignoring those critics who have argued that statements are unhelpful, as they focus attention on individual deficiencies rather than the whole-school approach e.g. Roaf and Bines, 1989; Ainscow, 1991a. The impression gained from the 1993 Education Act and the Code of Practice is that it has done little to alter the intrinsic values and principles of our special educational system. In addition, the original Code was implemented alongside substantial cuts in education budgets. Galloway, Armstrong and Tomlinson (1994) issued the following warning which is still pertinent today :

> The 1993 Act will make no changes to the funding arrangements for special educational provision, nor will it provide any additional resources ... Reducing the time [to complete statutory assessments] will not produce more resources. It will simply mean that bad decisions will be reached more quickly.

The general principle that children with special educational needs should – where this is what parents wanted – normally be educated in mainstream schools was enshrined into law by the 1993 Education Act and subsequently consolidated by the 1996 Education Act. Section 316A required maintained schools and LEAs to have regard to guidance on the statutory framework for inclusion. There is separate guidance to 'Inclusive Schooling – Children with Special Educational Needs' (DfES, 2001d) which provides advice on the practical operation of the new framework. It gives examples of the reasonable steps that maintained schools and LEAs could consider taking to ensure that the inclusion of a child with a statement of special educational needs in a mainstream schools is not incompatible with the efficient education of other children. The 2001 SEN and Disability Act delivers a strengthened right to inclusive education and has amended the 1996 Act and transformed the statutory framework for inclusion into a positive endorsement of inclusion. The 2001 Act also proposed a new Disability Rights Code of Practice for Schools to co-exist with the revised SEN Code of Practice which came into operation from January 2002.

A joint report by the Audit Commission and Ofsted (2002) analysed the problems LEAs have had in formulating and implementing coherent strategies for inclusion and draws some conclusions from the difficulties authorities have experienced. The main findings report that about one third of LEAs inspected in 2000/01 had unsatisfactory strategies for the inclusion of pupils with special needs. Consultation over the strategy for SEN in most authorities was thought but often too lengthy and frequently led to indecision. Generally LEA were clear about the principles underlying inclusion but vague on how to implement, especially regarding the transfer of resources, pupils who present with behavioural difficulties and the role of special schools. The report also commented that arrangements for the allocation of SEN funding were often unclear and obscured the respective accountability of schools and LEAs and that few LEAs had secure mechanisms for assessing the value added by their SEN provision.

The Definition, Identification and Measurement of Special Educational Needs

The 1981 Education Act marked a number of major changes. It referred to special educational needs as a subclass of the generality of special needs and rejected the categorical view of special educational needs, focusing instead upon the interactive, relative view. Circulars 8/81, 1/83 and 22/89 (DES, 1981, 1983, 1989a) which all offered advice to LEAs about the implementation of the Act, established that a child has special educational needs if he or she has a learning difficulty that:

is significantly greater than that of the majority of children of the same age (para. 4).

This has been criticised on both the grounds of circularity (Goacher et al., 1988) and vagueness (Gipps et al., 1985). The circularity of the definition is illustrated by the introduction of two other concepts, 'special educational provision' and 'learning difficulty', without precise meanings being attached to any of them. The 1993 Education Act retains the definition of special educational needs but recommends the general adoption of a five staged model for the assessment of SEN. Therefore an attempt has been made to provide guidance to reduce the circularity and vagueness. The increasing number of pupils with statements, reported in the Green Paper (DfEE, 1997b) and by the Audit Commission (2000), indicated that the initial criteria in the 1994 Code, about whether to initiate a statutory assessment, have had minimal impact.

The Warnock Report, Circular 8/81 and the Code of Practice all attempt to quantify the number of children who might be expected to fall within this group. It was felt that one child in every five at some time and one child in every six at any one time will require some form of special help. The Warnock Report looked at five sources of information on incidence of special needs:

* the Isle of Wight survey (Rutter et al. 1970),
* the Inner London Borough (ILB) study (Rutter et al. 1975; Berger et al. 1975),
* a study of children in the infant school (Webb, 1967),
* discussions with ILEA teachers (Inner London Education Committee, 1974) and
* the National Child Development Study (NCDS) (Pringle et al. 1966; Davie et al. 1972; Fogelman, 1976).

Gipps et al. (1985) split these sources into two groups – those which classified children according to measures of development and attainment regardless of the provision they were receiving, and those which classified children largely according to the provision they receive or it is thought they should receive. Thus, Rutter et al.'s Isle of Wight and ILB studies report the percentage of children, who, based on IQ and reading tests, behavioural rating and medical report were considered to have a problem in reading, have a psychiatric disorder, physical handicap or other severe problem. The NCDS data, on the other hand concerns the percentage of children receiving special help either in or out of ordinary schools, together with the percentage of children whom teachers thought would benefit from special help. With the exception of Rutter's ILB study all the reported prevalences were between 12 per cent and 20 per cent.

The 20 per cent figure is often quoted by LEA personnel as a baseline of provision to be aimed for. Dessent (1987) questions this notion of 20 per cent:

> If 'specialness' is judged in terms of educational failure and if educational success is synonymous with the possession of examination credentials – why stop at 20 per cent? Warnock's 20 per cent is but a short step from the '40 per cent' of pupils who leave our secondary school system with no negotiable qualifications after twelve years of compulsory schooling (p.21).

Further evidence for Dessent's uncertainty about the '20 per cent' is provided by the 1992 School Performance Tables (DfE, 1992b), which quoted 35 per cent of Y11 pupils who did not achieve at least one GCSE at grades A-C. Additionally, in 1978 HMI argued that up to 50 per cent of pupils in Scottish schools could be said to have learning difficulties (Scottish Education Department, 1978). In reality the wide currency of the 20 per cent figure is really a political compromise (Galloway, Armstrong and Tomlinson 1994, p13).

The other figure which has also gained wide currency – the two per cent has been examined by Gipps et al., 1985. They observed that as the special schools in London could accommodate only 1.5 per cent of the child population, this is where Burt advocated that the cut-off should be set. The figure of the two per cent is used in the 1994 Code of Practice:

> Only in a small minority of cases – nationally, around two per cent of children – will a child have special educational needs of a severity or complexity which requires the LEA to determine and arrange the special educational provision for the child by means of a statutory statement of special educational needs (para. 2:2).

An interesting insight into the thinking of the Warnock committee was made by Baroness Warnock when giving evidence to the select Education Committee which looked into aspects of special needs legislation to see how it is currently working (House of Commons Education Committee, 1993). In answering the question 'What percentage of children did you foresee would be covered by your statements at that time, or did you not have a percentage?' Baroness Warnock replied:

> We did not exactly, but we thought that it was roughly equivalent, possibly slightly fewer, than the 2 per cent of children who were then in special schools and we thought that probably the percentage might remain steady (para. 2).

At the time of publication of this book the most recent information on the incidence of statements taken from returns completed in January 2002 indicate a recorded range from 1.0 per cent in Nottinghamshire to 4.6 per cent in Telford and Wrekin (DfES, 2002c). This appears to highlight the lack of definition and agreement over what constitutes a prima facie case for full assessment. Goacher et al. (1988) reported that administrators in some LEAs spoke of 5 per cent as their target population for statements, while in others it was considered that 18 per cent could require a statement (p.53). Such figures contrast greatly with those LEAs who have pursued a policy of 'minimal statementing' e.g. Nottinghamshire (Gray and Dessent, 1993). Goacher et al. continue by stating these differences did not, therefore, reflect a misunderstanding of the concept of special educational needs in the 1981 Education Act, but were due more to a disagreement over what constituted the range of educational provision 'generally provided in schools, within the area of the local authority concerned' (Section 1(2) of the 1981 Education Act).

The Code of Practice on the identification and assessment of special educational needs has put further emphasis on 'the special needs pupil' discourse and places importance on early identification. The tensions between the different discourse areas will continually resurface during the course of this book, and subsequent Chapters will explore the conceptual confusion which is evident on the causes, nature and the solutions to the 'problem' of special educational needs.

The Reconceptualisation of Special Educational Needs

A number of commentators consider that a radical reconceptualisation of the state of provision for special needs is necessary (Dyson and Gains, 1993). They argue that educational thinking is moving from a focus on structures to a focus on processes and an emphasis on the practitioner as the main problem solver. However they contend that this shift is taking place before its implications are fully understood. The continued distinctions between 'special' and 'ordinary' needs, the continued existence of special needs teachers, of special needs departments in schools and of centralised local authority provision outside mainstream schools are all based on the structural approach. The two views are mutually incompatible and effectively sabotage each other. Dyson et al. (1994) examine case studies which suggest that some schools are addressing these tensions by developing an alternative model of provision. This model builds on the concept of the 'whole school approach' which has gradually evolved during the 1980s (Scottish Education Department, 1978; Inner London Education Authority, 1985), but also implies a reconceptualisation of teaching and learning. An emphasis is put on the examination and development of teaching styles across the curriculum, rather than on remediation of learning difficulties of individual children or the support of identified pupils within mainstream classes offering an otherwise unchanged pedagogy.

One way in which LEAs have attempted to manage the market for special education is to encourage and support schools to collaborate with each other to provide for special educational needs (Norwich et al., 1994). Also relevant to inter-school collaboration is Corwin's description of education systems as 'loosely coupled' (Corwin and Kerckhoff, 1981). This refers to the degree of autonomy of the interdependent elements (e.g. schools). This notion can be applied to the school system, by saying that there has been an increase in loose coupling following the government legislation (1988, 1993, 1996, 2001). The LEA's direct administrative role has been reduced in this context following the introduction of local management of schools or fair funding based on pupil-led funding.

Whilst accepting and agreeing with the main thrust of the 'reconceptualisation' movement, there are certain doubts about some of the practical issues which need to be addressed. First, it seems to this author, that on the whole education officers tend to work with the structures imposed upon them by elected members and central government. This point is illustrated by Galloway (1985):

> At local authority level, policy is influenced by political as well as educational considerations. Whether an LEA adopts a formal stance on such diverse issues as mixed ability teaching, corporal punishment and special educational needs depends as much on the political complexion and bias of its education committee members as on the interests and energy of the chief education officer and his (sic) senior colleagues.

While processes are clearly important, education officers might argue that one of their main roles is to enable the structures to work effectively and efficiently. The tendency noted by Dyson and Gains for LEAs to establish SEN support services since 1983 seems to emphasise this focus on structural thinking. Later in this book two LEAs will be used as case studies to illustrate their special educational needs policies and practice with particular regard to the allocation of non-SEN resources. One of the LEAs (*Mercia*) has adopted a process-oriented problem solving approach by using a professional audit to identify pupils experiencing special educational needs, which focuses on the arrangements made by schools. Although this methodology avoids the use of special needs categories, a centralised support team still exists to administer the audit and to provide general support to schools. There was no evidence in the schools of the alternative models of provision as reported by Dyson et al. (1994). They appeared to operate in the traditional mode of meeting special educational needs through a definite SEN department. The other LEA (*Whiteshire*) had a sophisticated network of support teams to meet the needs of pupils with statements. These support teams were mainly attached to local special schools thereby reinforcing categories of SEN and locating the ultimate responsibility for special needs provision outside the mainstream school.

The Education (Special Educational Needs) (Information) Regulations 1994 prescribe that schools must provide the name of the special educational needs coordinator (SENCO) or teacher responsible for the day-to-day operation of the SEN policy. The Code of Practice does acknowledge that in larger schools there may be an SEN coordinating or learning support team. However the Regulations have given emphasis to the term SENCO and with it the earlier way of thinking based on structures.

A similar argument could be made about the notion of collaboration between schools (e.g. Norwich et al. 1994). This idea sits uneasily with the competitive models based on the market encouraged by the local management of schools legislation. LEA advisory services have traditionally offered to schools in service training programmes which have involved consortia or clusters. The evidence for effective collaboration is particularly weak in the area of emotional and behavioural difficulties. There was a steady increase in the use of exclusion procedures leading to permanent alternative teaching arrangements such as home tuition (e.g. ACE, 1992; NUT, 1992; DfE, 1993c; Hayden, 1996). More recent statistics show that the number of permanent exclusions then declined for the 3 year period from 1997/98 but increased again in 2000/01 (DfES, 2002a). A partial explanation of the increase may be thought of as from the pressures brought about by the 1988 Education Act (Upton, 1992). Schools are now having to compete with each other for pupils and 'excellence' is likely to be viewed mainly in terms of position in performance tables of examination results. It is therefore understandable that school resources may be directed towards helping the more able and well-behaved pupils and not towards the more vulnerable.

In view of the major changes in educational policy since 1988, LEAs have gone through a transitional period with regard to their special needs policies. It is clear that there the deficiencies in the identification of and provision for pupils with special educational needs highlighted by the earlier reports from the Audit Commission/HMI (1992a and b) are still apparent even ten years later   (Audit Commission, 2002). Dyson and Gains' (1993) urge for a radical rethink within the whole area of special educational needs may partly have been a response to the longevity of the political Right, who were in power from 1979 to 1997. Within this context it is perhaps understandable that LEAs have continued with their structural thinking whilst keeping a weather eye on government legislation which has proffered the 'school failure' discourse. Realistically, until the government changes from an emphasis on the 'school failure' discourse and more to a view which encompasses evidence arising from the 'school and teacher effectiveness' research, then it is unlikely that the majority of LEAs and schools will reconceptualise their own policies.

The second part of this Chapter will now reflect on the main purposes for allocating additional resources for special educational needs.

The Purpose of Allocating Resources to Raise Educational Achievement

A first purpose for allocating additional funding for special educational needs is to raise educational achievement or to provide a focus on educational outcomes. The purpose is based on the view that pupils with various degrees of learning difficulty need more resources (i.e. they cost more) to educate to a given level of attainment e.g. to functional literacy. This can be seen as an effectiveness argument.

It is now commonplace, following the work of the Audit Commission (1985), to refer to the 'three E's' in education of economy, efficiency and effectiveness (Simkins, 1994). Chapter Three will make a further analysis of these and other principles which LEAs use to provide for pupils with special educational needs.

If the purpose for allocating additional funding for pupils with special educational needs is to raise achievement then the goals to be pursued could be defined in different ways. These might be defined as an improvement in National Curriculum attainments or perhaps for a special school pupil the emphasis would be on the independence/self help skills deemed to be necessary for life after compulsory schooling. The definition is important otherwise confusion will exist when the resource policy is evaluated. Knight (1993b) stresses the need for compatibility of aims between schools and LEAs. An example of incompatibility of *purpose* is where a school may use its non-statemented special educational needs funding to reduce class sizes for all pupils rather than targeting the resource towards those individual pupils who have been identified as experiencing special educational needs.

Dessent (1987, p51) makes the important point that resource policies are underpinned and guided by more fundamental ethical and value-based decisions concerning how *much* should be spent on *which* pupils in our schools. He describes the phenomenon of 'resource drift' whereby teaching or financial resources accorded to schools for SEN pupils drift over a period of time to other areas of the school's work which are perceived as having higher priority. The idea that children at the end of the continuum of need e.g. those who have profound/multiple learning difficulties (PMLD), require higher levels of individual attention would rarely be disputed. That they merit greater entitlement to teacher time and the available financial resources appears just within a society which expounds humanitarian ideals (Dessent, 1987, p55). This resourcing policy could be described as a form of positive discrimination although it is rarely conceptualised in this way by LEAs. However it does cause a conflict with the purpose of effectiveness. That is to say, some PMLD pupils will make very limited progress in terms of educational achievement during their compulsory education. The staffing levels allocated to these pupils would therefore appear to be more dependent on special care needs rather than special educational needs and have their roots in compassion and humanity (Pritchard, 1963).

In practice the principle of allocating additional resources for the purpose of raising the educational achievement of children with special needs has not been clearly distinguished from that of palliative care, compensation and positive discrimination.

For instance Ofsted (1993) reported that school development plans did not generally identify raising pupils' achievements as the central purpose of the establishments (para. 42). Historically the provision of additional resources for children with special needs has been strongly associated with providing them with more attention from teachers and para-teachers in an attempt to develop and refine intervention strategies for individual pupils. Ainscow (1993) argues that regrettably much less attention has been paid to conceptualising what we are trying to achieve or the effectiveness of the interventions.

The Purpose of Compensatory Resourcing

A different form of positive discrimination to the one described in the previous section, has its roots in the Plowden report (CACE, 1967) which itself was influenced by much of the anti-poverty legislation and programmes instituted in the USA during the 1960s (Silver and Silver, 1991). The Plowden report concluded from the research literature that evidence existed of strong links between educational achievement and a variety of students' home background characteristics (Sammons, 1992). It was argued that schools in socio-economically disadvantaged areas should be given extra resources because of the greater educational needs of their pupils.

One of Plowden's key proposals was the setting up of educational priority areas, the description of EPAs was far more neutral, although the evaluation, the social distance and the disapproval remained. Amongst Plowden's other recommendations were that incentives should be devised to attract and retain good teachers in 'problem areas' and for other special programmes, not just in education. The Plowden report focused on two main aspects of primary education: its endorsement of 'progressive' approaches to the primary school, and its clear recommendations for 'positive discrimination' and 'educational priority areas' as responses to economic, social, environmental and educational disadvantage. The Plowden committee drew energies from two important sources: firstly previous understandings of the relationship between education and disadvantage by its predecessor, the Hadow report (Board of Education, 1931) and other analyses of and policies relating to disadvantage since the 1930s, and secondly the recent British and international focus on poverty.

In the introduction of the Hadow report, the committee drew attention to Burt's evidence later reported in his 'The Backward Child' (Burt, 1937), that a 'squalid environment' had deleterious effects on physical and mental vitality. The committee also drew attention to 'a marked correspondence between the distribution of poverty and the distribution of educational retardation', the past underestimation of the effects of the environment, and the fact that a home in poverty did not give the young child the same educational start as did homes with more adequate means. These latter homes were described as those where children were encouraged to read and write, acquired greater general knowledge and 'the foundation of education':

For many young children from the poorest home all this is reversed. Their parents know very little of any life except their own, and have neither the time nor the leisure to impart what little they know. The vocabulary that the child picks up is restricted ... There is no literature that deserves the title...His universe is closed in by walls of brick and a pall of smoke ... (Board of Education, 1931, xix p54-58).

The Plowden committee's recommendation for 'positive discrimination' appears to have its roots in a Ministry of Education (1959b) volume of suggestions for primary teachers which contained a section on 'Special educational treatment', which contained the following passage:

> There are ... children who require special help because they have been severely deprived in their upbringing. If these do not respond to even a generous share of the teacher's attention it is clear that something more must be done for them (p.107).

The Plowden report provided a major stimulus for the development of policies of positive discrimination in the distribution of educational resources and, in particular, the use of educational priority indices (EPIs). The school remained central to the distribution of extra resources because the Plowden strategy had recommended using the experience of school as a means of compensating children for their disadvantages. Teachers working in schools with a high level of disadvantage received an additional amount of money known as the 'social priority allowance'.

Smith (1987) has argued that research studies and changing social conditions all contributed to making the educational priority area (EPA) an outdated concept. During the 1970s the arguments for positive discrimination by area gradually weakened and it was increasingly replaced by a policy of positive discrimination in favour of special groups or those with special needs. This trend is exemplified by the publication of two major reports Warnock in 1978 and Swann in 1985 (DES, 1985). The later was concerned with the educational needs of ethnic minorities. Educational disadvantage had effectively replaced EPAs (Smith, 1987).

The Plowden report concluded that home influences far outweighed those of the school. It drew on evidence comparable in many respects to that in the studies of Coleman (1966) and Jencks (1972). These two influential books from the United States argued that home background, including social class and economic class, were much more influential on a child's development than the effect of schooling. They reasoned that because the differences between families were much greater than those between schools, families were likely to exert the greater influence. As Mortimore et al. (1988) state:

Whilst it is undoubtedly true that an economically advantaged family – with comfortable housing, healthy diet, and time for stimulating educational experiences, contrasts starkly with an economically disadvantaged one – with inadequate, over-crowded or even a lack of permanent housing, poor diet and little time or money for educational experiences, it is also true that schools vary a great deal. The problem for researchers is how to tease out the effects of families from the effects of schools (p. 1).

A major criticism of compensatory resourcing is that no account is taken of the teacher and school effectiveness literature that is, schools do make a difference when dealing with pupils with learning and behavioural difficulties which can not be attributed to differences in the catchment area they served. Underachievement can therefore be viewed as both a curriculum and a funding issue. A fundamental question, which LEAs need to address, is how both of these two issues can be accommodated.

A second fundamental issue is that of accountability, which will be examined in Chapter Three. That is whether schools are spending the additional resources they are allocated for special educational needs on pupils or groups of pupils who are actually experiencing SEN and what they are achieving with these additional resources. Evans et al. (1994) provided evidence to suggest that schools were using SEN money to plug gaps in other budget areas or using the resources to create a regime supportive of children with social needs rather than targeting individuals or groups. If this continues to be the case then it is difficult to press for an increased level of SEN funding and a more finely tuned and targeted methodology of allocation. These arguments would become more convincing if LEAs and OFSTED inspectors were able to encourage Headteachers and governing bodies that the additional funding would be better utilised in focused curriculum based interventions and targeted towards groups and individuals which could then be open to evaluation. For example, schools could be asked by the LEA to prepare action plans about how and with whom they would use their non-statemented SEN allocation to enhance achievement in specific areas such as: reading and numeracy with the clear target of improving schools' average test scores at 7 and 11 e.g. Gross, (2000). The Ofsted report (1993) directed to access and achievement in urban education concluded that:

Curricular planning in the primary and secondary sectors particularly does not directly access the needs of children from disadvantaged backgrounds and does not focus sufficiently in raising their achievement (p. 6).

The next section will consider how significant research studies since the 1970s in the area of school and teacher effectiveness have had an important impact upon the concepts of special educational needs, educational disadvantage and the purpose of providing additional funding. It will demonstrate how the 'widespread pessimism about the extent that schools could have any impact on children's development' (Rutter et al., 1979), and Bernstein's (1970) view that 'Education cannot compensate for society', has been altered in the light of this school and teacher effectiveness research carried out during the 1970s and 1980s.

Research Studies on School and Teacher Effectiveness

Research on School Effectiveness and School Improvement

Since the mid 1980s there has been a burgeoning of interest in the twin fields of school effectiveness and school improvement by politicians, policy makers and practitioners (Stoll and Mortimore, 1995). The issue of differential school effectiveness whereby schools differ in their effectiveness for particular pupil groups has also gained in importance since the publication of school league tables has become mandatory (Sammons et al. 1993). Whilst it is acknowledged that no simple combination of factors produces an effective school, several reviewers have identified certain common processes and characteristics of more effective schools and those seen to have improved. Stoll and Mortimore contend that such factors provide a picture of what an effective school looks like but they cannot explain *how* the school became effective. This is the domain of school improvement. This section will now sample some of the literature from the area of school effectiveness and school improvement.

The slogan of the school effectiveness movement is that 'schools make a difference' (Brookhover et al., 1979). Wang, Haertel and Walberg (1990) undertook a comprehensive review of research on variables related to learning. They examined 228 items related to school learning and consulted 179 authoritative research and review papers. The analysis confirmed the relative strength of the influence of factors such as : metacognition, classroom management, quality of instruction, classroom interactions and climate, and the peer group. Compared with these factors, district demographics such as per-pupil expenditure and contractual limits on class size, and school and district policies (e.g. on discipline or home-school contact) were much less influential. The authors state:

The items most important to learning outcomes were those directly tied to students' engagement with the material learned.

The research demonstrated that student aptitude characteristics were the most important of six broad categories of influence. Important characteristics were students' capacities to plan, monitor and review their learning strategies (metacognitive processes), their general intelligence, competence in reading and mathematics and verbal ability (cognitive processes), their constructive attitudes and behaviour (social and behavioural attributes) and their motivation. Classroom Instruction and Climate had nearly as much impact: classroom management (e.g. smooth transitions, teacher 'withitness', and learner accountability); student-teacher interactions (frequency and quality); quantity of instruction; classroom climate (e.g. clear goals and a clear academic focus); classroom instruction (e.g. systematic sequencing of material, use of review, guided student practice and the use of feedback and correctives); and classroom implementation and support (which includes the contribution of in-service training to improving teachers' skills). The out-of-school context was also relatively important: home environment and parental support, community influences and extra-curricular activities.

Programme Design had a moderate influence: well designed textbooks, appropriate grouping and activities well aligned to goals. School organisation was also moderately influential: school culture, teacher involvement in decision-making, parental involvement in the school and school demographics and policies (e.g. size of school and number of support teachers), for example District and State characteristics were among the least influential.

Edmonds (1982) has noted the following features that seem to be characteristic of exceptional schools:

• The principal's leadership and attention to the quality of instruction.
• A pervasive and broadly understood instructional focus.
• An orderly, safe climate conducive to teaching and learning.
• Teacher behaviours that convey the expectation that all students are expected to obtain at least minimum mastery.
• The use of measures of pupil achievement as the basis for programme evaluation.

These rather general features have been confirmed by an impressive range of other studies (e.g. Rutter et al., 1979; Purkey and Smith, 1983; Bickel and Bickel, 1986; Mortimore et al., 1988; Smith and Tomlinson,

1989). Reynolds (1990) identification of important factors included site management, leadership, staff stability, curriculum organisation, staff development, maximised learning time, recognition for academic success, and parental involvement in school. These factors are associated in effective schools with the following process characteristics within the culture of the school: collaborative planning, a sense of community, clear expectations shared among staff, and firm order and discipline. The factors are summed up by Rutter, who when commenting on the factors which make good schools, noted it is:

> ... schools which set good standards, where the teachers provide good models of behaviour, where they (the pupils) are praised and given responsibility, where general conditions are good and where the lessons are well-conducted (p. 204).

More recently, there has also been a debate over the question of differential effectiveness, that is whether or not schools do better for pupils with particular characteristics. Nuttall et al. (1989) found evidence of differential school effectiveness although Jessen and Gray (1991) argued that there was no conclusive evidence for it. Work by Sammons et al. (1993) has showed more support for the existence of differential school slopes and have argued that this has significant policy implications for the publication of schools' examination and test results.

Sammons et al. (1995) have reviewed the British and North American research literature and have provided a summary of eleven key factors or correlates of effectiveness. These are participatory leadership, shared vision and goals, teamwork, a learning environment, emphasis on teaching and learning, high expectations, positive reinforcement, monitoring and enquiry, pupil rights and responsibilities, learning for all and partnerships and support. Sammons et al. acknowledge that the list is neither exhaustive nor are the factors necessarily independent of each other. The authors share an elaborate view of causality in that schools and classrooms are complex, non-linear, adaptive systems and that rules of simple cause and effect can not be applied.

However the review has been criticised by Hamilton (1995), who proposes that research into effective schooling has become too product oriented and is pulled by the market place rather than steered by axioms and principles.

> I reject both the suppositions and conclusions of such research. I regard it as an ethnocentric pseudo-science that serves to mystify anxious administrators and marginalise classroom practitioners. Its UK manifestations are shaped not so

much by inclusive educational values that link democracy, sustainable growth, equal opportunities and social justice but, rather by a divisive political discipline redolent of performance-based league tables and performance-related funding (Hamilton, 1995).

This example again demonstrates the tensions apparent when following different discourses of special educational needs. The notion of effectiveness will be explored again in Chapter Three when an investigation will take place of the principles which LEAs use to provide additional resources for pupils with SEN. In summary, there appears to be a fine dividing line between the benefits of taking the emphasis off individual child deficits by considering context factors and 'peddling simplistic school effectiveness snake oil as a cure-all' (Reynolds, 1995).

Research on Teacher Effectiveness

Until recently most of the school effectiveness studies have focused on school level factors (Stoll and Mortimore, 1995) yet it is clear that school and classroom development need to be linked. Wang et al.'s review of the research considered teacher effectiveness and as well as school effectiveness. The comments which follow, relating more specifically to teacher effectiveness, will to some extent overlap with some of Wang et al.'s overall conclusions. Generally Ainscow (1991b) suggests that there seems to a general consensus of findings within the research literature (e.g. Bennett, 1991; Bickel and Bickel, 1986; Brophy, 1983; Rosenshine, 1983). Rosenshine (1971) was one of the first to note that data from different investigations using different methods indicated that certain teacher behaviours were consistently correlated with student achievement gain. A more recent synthesis of the findings in this area of research is provided by Porter and Brophy (1988). They suggest that the research provides a picture of effective teachers as semi-autonomous professionals who:

- are clear about their instructional goals;
- are knowledgeable about their content and the strategies for teaching it;
- communicate to their students what is expected of them - and why;
- make expert use of existing instructional materials in order to devote more time to practices that enrich and clarify the content;
- are knowledgeable about their students, adapting instruction to their needs and anticipating misconceptions in their existing knowledge;
- teach students metacognitive strategies and give them opportunities to master them;

- address higher – as well as lower-level cognitive objectives;
- monitor students' understanding by offering regular appropriate feedback;
- integrate their instruction with that in other subject areas;
- are thoughtful and reflective about their practice.

Ainscow (1991b) has compared Porter and Brophy's findings with those of Ainscow and Muncey (1989). Ainscow and Muncey were concerned with policies for meeting special needs in ordinary schools. Within their project the most effective teachers:

- emphasis the importance of meaning;
- set tasks that are realistic and challenging;
- ensure that there is progression in children's work;
- provide a variety of learning experiences;
- give pupils opportunities to choose;
- have high expectations;
- create a positive atmosphere;
- provide a consistent approach;
- recognise the efforts and achievements of their pupils;
- organise resources to facilitate learning;
- encourage pupils to work co-operatively;
- monitor progress and provide regular feedback.

Ainscow (1991b) uses this evidence to support the view that teachers said to be successful in meeting special needs are to a large extent using strategies that help all pupils to experience success. As Stoll (1991) argues :

> ... in an effective school with quality classroom instruction, all children, irrespective of social class differences, can make more progress than all children in an ineffective school with poor teaching methods.

Conclusions

This Chapter set out to discover how the conceptualisation of SEN impacts upon both the policy and purposes of providing additional funding. There has been much confusion by policy makers about the definition and the overlap between SEN and social disadvantage (Lee, 1995). I shall now examine how the two policy discourses of the 'special needs pupil' and 'school and teacher effectiveness' map onto the two main purposes of SEN funding i.e. effectiveness and equity. A first analysis of this problem might suggest that the purpose of effectiveness maps more readily to the 'special needs pupil' discourse and the purpose of equity is linked closely to the 'school and teacher effectiveness' discourse. However I think this is an oversimplification of the case and that in fact both discourses address effectiveness and equity but with different emphases.

If an LEA wishes to follow only the 'special needs pupil' discourse then the purposes of raising achievement of individual pupils (effectiveness) and allocating resources to individual pupils (equity/equality of opportunity) become all important. On the other hand, the outcome of following the 'school and teacher effectiveness' discourse is to place more value upon raising achievement of *all* pupils (effectiveness) by allocating resources to particular schools (compensatory resourcing). The implication of this finding is that LEAs may wish to adopt both purposes and both policy discourses within their formula funding arrangements. An important strategy for designing a SEN funding formula is the combination of the purposes and policy discourses by allocating distinct and separate amounts for different formula components.

A number of writers e.g. Dyson and Gains (1993), have suggested that a radical rethink about SEN is necessary, however this is unlikely to happen due to inevitable governmental time constraints. It is significant that the new Labour government in 1997 published a White Paper (DfEE, 1997a) and a Green Paper (DfEE, 1997b) within the first five months of taking office. The 'school failure' discourse was still to be found in the White Paper and the 'special needs pupil' discourse remained the focal point of the Green Paper and also the revised Code of Practice in 2001. Disappointedly the government's 1998 Programme of Action (DfEE, 1998a) has been based on the present educational structures involving a revised Code of Practice rather than, for instance, a radical reappraisal of the system of 'statementing' e.g. Audit Commission, 2002. In this context many LEAs, who are continuing to struggle with escalating SEN budgets, are inevitably finding that their solutions to the problem leads them further down the 'special needs pupil' road e.g. by adopting stricter criteria for the identification of pupils with SEN to be considered for a statutory assessment. It may take a major change in the way that resources are 'attached' to statements to halt the statutory assessment momentum and to shift the emphasis more towards the 'school and teacher effectiveness' discourse.

However on a more positive note, it is salutary to remember that in the UK the right to education for all children with SEN was not recognised until the 1970 Education Act. The principles and practice relating to SEN have therefore developed more during the last 25 years than have those in most other areas of education (Wedell, 1993).

Chapter Three

Funding Principles

Whether LEAs seek to pursue the purpose of raising educational achievement or of compensation or seek to address both purposes, there are a range of objectives or principles which provide criteria against which different methods of allocating resources for special educational needs can be assessed in order to determine the preferred set of methods. In this Chapter an examination is carried out of the range of objectives or principles which LEAs need to address when determining their method of allocating resources for special and inclusive education.

The next Chapter will consider in greater detail the relevant government circulars pertaining to Fair Funding. To summarise the government does not prescribe a uniform formula but the expectation is for LEAs in preparing and reviewing their formulae to bear in mind certain general principles. The general principles or rules of formula funding are summarised in the DfEE consultation paper on Fair Funding (DfEE, 1998b). Seven principles are listed which the Government believes should determine the form of the new financial framework : Standards, Self-management, Accountability, Transparency, Opportunity, Equity and Value for Money.

This Chapter will consider some of these principles or criteria and suggest others by which a funding formula should be evaluated. The principles are listed below and have been drawn from three sources: Ross 1983); Levačić (1995); Ross and Levačić (1999).

1. Simplicity. A simple formula will assist transparency and will also help to keep administrative costs low.
2. Equity. This principle also includes objectivity in the distribution and differentiation of resources.
3. Effectiveness: what do the additional resources achieve and how does this relate to the intentions of the policy makers? This principle includes the issue of how to relate resource allocation to individual needs.
4. Responsiveness to needs. The distribution formula should be sufficiently needs responsive to reflect the continuum and range of SEN.

5. Efficiency and value for money. This principle includes discussion of the 'resource paradox' whereby schools which raise their educational achievement will receive a reduction in funding if the SEN index is based on measures of educational achievement which the school can influence.
6. Stability of funding.
7. Cost containment and the need to reduce and stabilise the rate of statements.
8. Accountability. The Audit Commission (1994) emphasise the need to ensure that schools are aware of the amount they receive for pupils with special educational needs through their normal allocation under formula funding and that they should account for how this money is spent.

The listing and descriptions of evaluative criteria take a technical perspective which is crucial to understanding the resource implications of Fair Funding. However other perspectives could have been considered which are not developed in this Chapter, such as the micro-political or a cultural perspective (Levačić, 1995). I have adopted the technical perspective because it seems to me that it offers valuable insights which complement the discourses of the 'special needs pupil' and the 'school and teacher effectiveness'.

An important point to note at this stage is that these objectives are not mutually exclusive and some are better delivered by some types of SEN allocation system than others. For example free school meals is one of the best SEN indicators for the objective of simplicity and low administrative cost but performs poorly with respect to responsiveness to individual need. Each of the criteria will now be examined individually.

Simplicity

The 'simplicity rule' is intended to make resource allocation more widely understood and transparent. The difficulties in understanding complicated formulae is amply illustrated by the following comment made in a House of Commons select committee (House of Commons Education Committee, 1994) by an education officer giving evidence about the construction of a Common Funding Formula:

> The difficulty we have is that the system starts with Standard Spending
> Assessments. Really I can stop there in terms of problems because once
> you start laying complexity upon a system which is probably understood

by three people in the country, and I have to say that I have never met any of those...(para. 35).

Although, as Lee (1992b) argues the aim is commendable, it demands that LEAs adopt simple solutions to what are inherently extremely complicated problems. Additionally the 'simplicity rule' does not integrate well with some of the other objectives e.g. responsiveness to individual need, as recommended by the Code of Practice. This is especially the case if an LEA is concerned with the purpose of raising educational achievement.

ILEA (Sammons et al., 1983) devised an Educational Priority Index (EPI) and demonstrated the impact of 'cumulative disadvantage'. That is, there is clear evidence that pupils who experience several forms of disadvantage are affected in a cumulative rather than an additive way. This is illustrated in Table 3.1.

Table 3.1   Percentage of Secondary Pupils with Different Combinations of Characteristics in Verbal Reasoning Band 3

Combination of Characteristics	% of Pupils in Verbal Reasoning Band 3
No factors	10.8
Eligibility for Free Meals only	21.1
Large Families only	13.0
Parental Occupation only	18.4
Free Meals and Parental Occupation	26.7
Free Meals, Parental Occupation and Large Families	31.8

Source : Sammons et al., 1983.

Table 3.1 shows that only 11 per cent of secondary pupils within verbal reasoning band 3 were not affected by any of the EPI factors. However, if eligibility for free meals is considered, 21 per cent of pupils were identified by this measure alone but the figure rose to 32 per cent when free meals was combined with the characteristics of parental occupation and large families. The EMIE survey (Marsh, 2002) has shown that 96 per cent of LEAs use free school meals data in some form and that 82 per cent of LEAs are using two or more indicators of additional or special educational needs formula elements in their resource allocation. The use of Free School Meals (FSM) information has been chosen by LEAs as it meets the criterion of simplicity, is readily available and is administratively cheap to use. (Section 45 of the 1988 Education Act requires LEAs to collect information regarding the entitlement to free school meals).

Although the above comments have highlighted some of potential difficulties in adopting the 'simplicity rule', nevertheless it is important to remember that:

> ... the old system , as familiar as it was inequitable and ineffective, was also guilty of failing those very same children ... LMS did not cut short a 'golden age' of special education. (Lee, 1992c, p296).

Equity

Dyson (2001) contends that the special needs system is flawed as a means of delivering equity and proposes a move away from the individualisation approach towards the development of systemic interventions embedded in mainstream schools and classrooms. This section will explore the intriguing concept of equity in greater detail (Lee, 1995, 1996). It may be broadly equated with 'fairness' and 'justice' (Le Grand, 1991, Ch.2). The term can also be defined as relating to the fairness with which different people or different categories of people are treated in relation to the distribution of resources they receive (Levačić, 1995). One useful distinction is that between procedural equity and distributional equity. Procedural equity refers to the consistent application of agreed rules. It can therefore be argued that the allocation of non-statemented special educational needs resources by means of quantitative indicators of need, as in the prescribed LMS/Fair Funding formula, is procedurally equitable in comparison with former methods of allocating resources to schools. These former methods depended to some extent on LEA officer discretion and hence on head teachers' ability to exploit their networks for the benefit of their individual schools. This procedural justification for formula funding was clearly stated in Circular 7/88:

> it (the formula) should be based on an assessment of schools' objective needs, rather than on historic patterns of expenditure in order to ensure that resources are allocated equitably (DES, 1988a, para. 22).

Circular 7/88 further claimed that an objective approach ensures 'an equitable allocation of the available resources' (para. 99). Again the aim is commendable but in practice has caused some confusion over the interpretation of what is meant by an 'objective' formula. As Simkins (1994) states:

> On the one hand, it might simply imply that the formula is specified so that its outcome can be predicted once the values of the independent variables are known. Alternatively, and more demandingly, it might mean that there is a clearly defined rationale for its components. Evidence suggests that the early days of formula funding have been dominated by the former interpretation (p. 17).

The crucial test for the distinction between objective and subjective data initially appeared to be whether the data can be collected without any aspect of judgement by headteachers, teachers, educational psychologists or any other LEA staff. Internal professional audits of pupils' needs were not acceptable at first to the Department for Education and Science (DES) as they were deemed too subjective. The government Department have since revised their views, particularly in the light of the Code of Practice, and now accept properly moderated audits of need e.g. Kent and Northamptonshire.

Distributional equity is the form of equity which most people associate with the concept of social justice. It refers to the distribution of income and wealth and the means to obtain these. Distributional equity is a particularly important concept for education given that children's educational attainment is unevenly distributed and is positively associated with social background factors. Le Grand and Bartlett (1993) suggested that an appropriate distributional equity criterion for assessing an allocation system is the extent to which it distributes resources according to need rather than to other factors such as income and social status.

There are two forms of distributional equity: horizontal and vertical. Horizontal equity is the principle that every individual in like circumstances should receive the same treatment. The guidelines listed in Circular 7/88 strongly support horizontal equity principles i.e. the importance given to age-weighted pupil units and that, except for very small schools, the budget share must be based on average LEA teacher costs rather than actual costs. Vertical equity is the principle that individuals who have different needs should be treated in ways which compensate for these differences. The criterion that the special needs resource allocation system should be responsive to individuals' differentiated needs is an application of the vertical equity principle. By adhering to the 'simplicity rule' Circular 7/88 advises against vertical equity by stating that the use of a 'multiplicity of factors':

...will make the formula less intelligible without necessarily making it more equitable (para. 104).

Allocating resources according to special needs audits conducted by special needs co-ordinators and headteachers, as in Kent and Northamptonshire, fulfils the vertical equity criterion, but needs to be carefully moderated to ensure that horizontal equity is achieved as well, so that children with similar needs in different schools get similarly resourced. The professional audit approach with its subjective element performs less well against the procedural equity criterion and against the principle of cost containment and the need to stabilise the rate of statements. There has been a continuing increase in statements over a number of years in both Kent and Northamptonshire. Following local government reorganisation in 1998 the increase in the number of statements in England reduced to 0.4 per cent from 1999 to 2002 however, there was a 10 per cent increase in Kent and a 11 per cent increase in Northamptonshire during the same time period (DfES, 2002c).

Simkins (1995) argues that the Government's rationale for its educational reforms, commencing with the 1988 Education Reform Act made no explicit reference to equity, however it is unlikely that these reforms will be neutral in equity terms. He draws on the work of Wise (1967) and Monk (1990) to divide distributional equity into two broad categories: input based and outcome based.

The first category, which defines equity in terms of resource inputs, comprises:

* the 'equal expenditure per pupil' definition;
* the 'maximum variance' definition: placing a limit on the permitted variance in expenditure per pupil;
* the 'foundation' definition: a prescribed minimum level of expenditure provided for all pupils;
* the 'classification' definition: treating equally all members of specified categories i.e. horizontal equity; whether these be defined in terms of need, ability to benefit or some other variable; and also allocating more to those with greater needs (vertical equity).

Such expenditure-based approaches are attractive in policy terms and most LEAs surveyed by Lee (1992a) could be classified using the four input-based criteria. However these approaches do not address the accountability issues of the relationship between expenditure, educational processes and learning outcomes. In an attempt to incorporate some view about the outcomes to which the resources are intended to contribute, Wise (1967) suggested the four following definitions of equity:

- the 'minimum attainment' definition: sufficient resources should be provided to enable all pupils to reach a minimum level of attainment;
- the 'full opportunity' definition: resources should continue to be provided until the marginal gains of all pupils are reduced to zero;
- the 'levelling' definition: resources should be distributed so that the least disadvantaged are favoured most and variances in achievement are minimised;
- the 'competition' definition: resources should be provided in proportion to the pupils' ability to benefit i.e. marginal benefit per unit of resource which is the same for all pupils.

Simkins (1995) has integrated the input and outcome based definitions together and has argued that they fall into three categories (see Table 3.2).

Table 3.2   Definitions of equity

	Input-based	Outcome-based
Equality	Equal expenditure (strong) Maximum variance (weak)	
Baseline	Foundation	Minimum attainment
Differential	Classification	Full opportunity Competition Levelling

Source : Simkins, 1995.

The definitions of equity illustrate the relationship between the principle of equity and the purpose of providing additional funding for pupils with special educational needs. Simkins asserts that the input-based definitions (equal expenditure and maximum variance) are more concerned with resource equality than with equity. In other words they ensure that all pupils are treated the same rather than treated fairly. Lee (1992a) has shown that a large number of LEAs used the 'equal expenditure' definition in the first generation of SEN formulae, by allocating a unit cost to free school meals data. One example of the second of Simkins' categories, i.e. of outcome-based baseline criteria, is found by the Government's performance indicators for Key Stage 4 which records the number of pupils for each school achieving 5 or more GCSEs with a level A to C. However this definition does not provide any rationale for determining the different levels of expenditure required to achieve the minimum level of attainment.

It has already been argued in Chapter Two that if the LEA's purpose for providing additional funding for special educational needs is to raise achievement, then differentiation of costs is important. Examples of differential equity are provided within Simkins' third category of definitions. The 'full opportunity' definition appears to focus on the much quoted policy of 'the need to maximise pupil achievement' or 'enabling a pupil to achieve his or her potential'. Monk (1990) has argued that this definition is flawed because of the difficulties of putting the policy into practice as it places almost unlimited demands on resources without providing guidance about distribution if resources are finite. Also, the equity consequences are potentially damaging if pupils' ability to benefit varies significantly. The remaining two differential definitions of equity, 'competition' and 'levelling' are important because of the implications. As Simkins (1995) states:

> If we assume that there is a fixed quantity of resources to be allocated and that pupils have different capacities to benefit in terms of learning from a given level of resourcing, then there is a clear choice available. We can attempt to maximise the total learning gain by directing resources to those whom we expect to gain the most even though this may widen the distribution of learning outcomes (the 'competition', 'élitist' or 'utilitarian' approach); or we can direct resources to those whom we judge to be most disadvantaged, thus hopefully reducing the level of variance in individual learning outcomes but at the potential cost of a lower total level of learning for the whole group (the 'levelling' or justice as fairness' approach).

The outcome-based definitions of equity have a clear relationship with the principle of effectiveness. That is to say maximising pupil outcomes (full opportunity), ensuring minimum standards (levelling) or maximising 'value added' (competition), all imply different resource allocations.

It is debatable whether the 'competition' definition can really be considered as a concept of equity at all. In practice however many examples are apparent, for example within the area of specific learning difficulties (SpLD). Riddell et al. (1994) reports of a study which focused on a group of parents of children experiencing SpLD in Scotland. The research found that within this group, parents with middle-class occupational levels were: three times more likely than working-class parents to report that the special educational provision their child received were inadequate; more likely to seek additional private tuition, but were 'able to secure a disproportionate share of additional provision within the state sector'. Similarly, research by Gross (1996) found that pupils with SpLD were more likely to be 'overfunded' than other types of learning difficulties. Croll and Moses (1985) report that teachers attribute the source of children's difficulties to IQ, other within child variables, or the home background, but very rarely the school itself. This finding might explain the viewpoint held by some teachers that SpLD pupils are more 'worthy' of additional resources than their moderate learning difficulty (MLD) counterparts, as their higher abilities would enable them to make better progress. The issue whether expectations for future attainment of SpLD pupils can reasonably be based on measured IQ is seriously questioned by Stanovich (1994), Stanovich and Siegal (1994) and Fletcher et al. (1994). These researchers provide clear evidence that it is not possible to distinguish between SpLD and poor readers on significant measures of their reading skills or response to teaching. The issue of differential equity will be considered again in Chapter Five.

An understanding of the various concepts of equity is important during formula construction, because LEAs can implement various policy thrusts by their selection of factors and different weightings. There is also an additional equity consideration related to the 'geographical lottery' aspect of variation between LEAs of the funding of both statemented and non-statemented SEN. The Government's stress on procedural equity and horizontal equity i.e. age weighted pupil units has placed an over emphasis on the criterion of age being the most important determinant of need. LEAs which have developed professional audits of need have attempted to balance these effects by introducing a vertical equity component. These examples are all 'input-based'. Chapter Five will include an exploration of 'output-based' approaches which, as Simkins (1995) suggests, would address more explicitly the relationships between resource deployment and pupil achievement and provides a direct link with the principle of effectiveness.

Effectiveness

Chapter One has already considered the principle of effectiveness in relation to the purpose of allocating resources to raise educational achievement and in particular from the discourse of teacher and school effectiveness e.g. Sammons et al. (1994), Hutchison (1993). The effectiveness of a funding formula will depend on the extent to which the formula delivers central and local authority aims for education (Levačić, 1989). The increasing requirement for accountability from the education service is closely connected to demands for greater effectiveness since educators are facing growing expectations that they should be able to demonstrate that they have used resources effectively (and efficiently). This criterion is now one of the four aspects of a school's performance that is assessed in the Ofsted (1995b, 1995c, 1995d, 1999b) Guidance on Inspection. One of the contributing factors to this assessment is the school's special educational needs provision.

As has already been stressed, any assessment of effectiveness depends crucially on the objectives that have been set and against which what is provided or what is achieved educationally is assessed. Simkins (1994) suggests that the most obvious way to explore effectiveness in education is to address the issue of pupil learning. The principle of effectiveness is a highly relevant criterion if the purpose of additional resources for children with special educational needs is to raise their educational achievement. It then becomes important, in order to assess effectiveness and render accountability for effectiveness to define what is meant for individual pupils by the objective of 'raising achievement'. Also of importance is the choice and the validity of the indicators which are used within the formula, which will be discussed further in Chapter Five.

Responsiveness To Needs

Amongst the issues to emerge from the national reports which have been published following the implementation of the 1981 Education Act are the relationship between non-statemented and statemented special educational needs, the resources to meet SEN generally, together with the increasing demand for pupils to be statemented. There appears to be a strong case for the systematic allocation of teaching time to meet the wider range of SEN to enable appropriate provision for this wider range to be made and to reduce the excessive pressure which may otherwise be placed on LEAs to carry out full assessments and make statements. It has been clear from DfES circulars that the LEAs' policy for SEN must cover the wider range of SEN and not just the arrangements for pupils with statements.

The Warnock Report placed great emphasis on the continuum of needs. As mentioned above, Dessent (1987) has argued that typically resources are allocated in a discontinuous way to a continuum of needs (p.55). This is particularly apparent when Circular 11/90 is considered in parallel with LEA's non-statemented resources. A primary aged pupil with a statement at band 5 within a special school, i.e. other learning difficulties, can accrue 0.1 teacher time and 0.1 teaching assistant (TA) time (approximately

£4,900 at year 2002 costs with on-costs). A secondary aged special school pupil at band 5 can accrue 0.1 teacher and 0.05 TA time (approximately £4,000 at year 2002 costs). Within the same LEA a band 5 mainstream pupil with a statement would typically be resourced with 0.1 of an outreach teacher or approximately £3,000. However a non-statemented primary SEN pupil in this LEA would attract £450 and a secondary non-statemented pupil £900.

LEAs which have adopted an audit approach may have already extended the five bands of statemented resourcing to include bands for non statemented special educational needs pupils. For example as part of their overall SEN funding approach, Kent continue to allocate money based on their audit of special needs . However because of perverse incentives (see next section on efficiency) whereby schools dramatically increased the numbers of pupils on the SEN register, Kent are now transferring money out of the SEN audit budget to factors using prior attainment and social deprivation proxies.

Table 3.3   Audit Allocation in Kent per primary pupil with SEN but without a statement 1996/97 compared to 2002/2003

Level	1996/97	2002/03
2	£390	£220
3	£740	£450

If the main purpose of allocating additional resources for special educational needs is to raise educational achievement and provide access to the curriculum then it might be expected that differentiated levels of resourcing should be provided for pupils with different levels and types of need. A significant proportion of statements are produced for pupils with specific learning difficulties. In *Mercia* 32 per cent of all statements issued in one year were written for pupils experiencing specific learning difficulties. Therefore special consideration needs to be taken that the formula identifies the full range of special educational needs. Relationships have been cited at a school level for the numbers of pupils taking free school meals and the numbers having special educational needs (e.g. McConville et al., 1991). However the relationship between free school meals and specific learning difficulties is less clear. The issue of different SEN indicators will be explored in greater detail in Chapter Five.

The principle of responsiveness of the allocation system to individual need is thus highly complex and conflicts with the principle of simplicity and low administrative costs.

Efficiency

Efficiency has been defined as the achievement of given outcomes at least cost. The salience of the efficiency principle depends on the purpose of the resource allocation. If compensation for social disadvantage is the main purpose then efficiency and value for money would not be important criteria, whereas they would be if raising achievement is the main purpose. However if the purpose of additional funding is for effectiveness reasons then further implications exist for the LEA which are usefully discussed in the context of the purchaser-provider model.

The purchaser-provider model used here is one in which the purchaser and provider functions are undertaken by separate organisations e.g. LEA and schools. The aim of separating the purchaser role from that of the provider is to prevent 'provider capture', i.e. to prevent suppliers of services from having a monopoly. In economic theory a monopoly is against the interests of clients as it has no incentive to provide services at an efficient cost or of the quality desired by its customers and therefore operates in the interests of the providers rather than those of the customers. This model needs to be distinguished from the 'traditional state welfare bureaucracy model' in which the purchaser and provider functions are undertaken by the same organisation e.g. the LEA.

The Audit Commission report (1992a) suggested that the purchaser-provider model could be used to allocate resources for pupils with SEN. That is, LEAs could purchase services from schools on behalf of children with special educational needs. In some circumstances the LEAs will be the providers and the schools the purchasers. For example, if the LEA delegates the funding for support services to schools and leaves schools to buy in those services which they feel they need, then the school is purchasing from the LEA. In the context of non-statemented special educational needs resource allocation then the LEA, as a provider of additional resources, might expect a higher level of efficiency if resources are allocated for raising educational achievement in well defined outcome terms than when the purpose is for compensation.

A further aspect of the efficiency criterion is the issue of the 'resource paradox' or 'perverse incentives' whereby a school which raises its academic achievements will be penalised if an index of its educational output is included in the formula for funding special educational needs. An allocation system which discourages schools from striving for the highest possible educational attainment for their students would be inefficient as well as ineffective. However if attainment is measured at intake to primary or secondary school, the danger of rewarding low performing schools can be overcome.

Another issue with respect to incentives is whether the allocation system gives schools sufficient incentive to recruit, retain and provide for SEN pupils. If schools perceive that the costs of such pupils outweigh the benefits to the school then the allocation system is not promoting efficiency from the perspective of LEA SEN policy. The issue of the perceived benefits to a school of having SEN pupils is related not only to the financial incentives but also to the school's educational values and aims. It has been suggested by Lunt and Evans (1994) that a 'place element', as recommended by the Touche Ross (1990) report on LMSS would, if incorporated into a funding formula with a pupil element as well, give schools a greater incentive to assume responsibility for pupils experiencing special educational needs.

Stability of Funding

Another important principle of formula funding is that of stability in order for financial planning to occur and so that least disruptions are caused to individual schools. This is emphasised in Circular 7/88 which stated that the formula must be:

> ... simple, clear and **predictable** ... so that governors, head teachers, parents and the community can understand how it operates and why it yields the results it does, and can include it as a key factor in their **planning for future years** (para. 104) (my emphasis).

The LMS Initiative (1992) reported that the majority of LEAs responding to their survey claimed that the most important criterion in designing their formula had been to 'minimise change'. This is perhaps understandable given the wish by LEAs to minimise 'winners' and 'losers' and to prevent the disequilibrium that large discrepancies would cause. Moreover, the study reports that even in the minority of LEAs that claim to have taken the opportunity to change funding patterns to reflect more objective measures of need, it is likely that the impact on individual schools was scrutinised heavily before this course of action was taken. The LMS Initiative felt that this finding was disappointing in that it would appear to conflict with the principle that resource allocation under LMS should be based on 'objectively measured needs' rather than historical levels of funding. However for many LEAs such a distinction was a false dichotomy.

> For them, historical funding did reflect need – indeed when it came to designing the formula there was no better objective measure of need than the previous pattern of funding, which in itself had risen through an accumulation of LEA decisions over time and in response to educational need. Thus the attempt to match history could be interpreted as an attempt to match need (LMS Initiative, 1992).

Despite the attempts of LEAs to minimise changes in the funding to individual schools, the move to formula funding has caused a redistribution of resources. Thomas and Bullock (1992) reported that the frequency of budget losses (comparing formula and historic funding for the same set of variables) is greater among small schools in both primary and secondary sectors than in larger schools. The LMS Initiative survey found that the maximum gain for any individual school was 91 per cent of its previous budget figure and the maximum loss 61 per cent (51 per cent and 34 per cent respectively after dampening and transitional arrangements). In terms of sectors and types of schools, the survey found there had been a shift from the secondary sector to the primary sector and from small or under occupied schools to large schools. Therefore the main gainers were large primary schools and large secondary schools and the main losers were small secondary schools and under occupied schools. The same association with budget loss and size, particularly in the secondary sector, is reported by Levačić (1992) for 16 LEAs. The studies referred to drew data from a large number of LEAs but were only able to use statistical data on a narrow range of school characteristics. Levačić (1993) focused on a single LEA and was able to analyse a wider range of school level data and interpret the findings using detailed knowledge of the LEA's formula. She found that whilst the largest determinant of budget changes was the change in pupil numbers, schools with high unit costs due to excess capacity or being relatively small tended to lose budget. Thus the formula promoted cost efficiency by reducing the number of schools which had large positive discrepancies between their unit costs and the average for their sector.

The LMS Initiative report emphasised the importance of the formula for transmitting policy signals to schools. However the report also offered the warning that it is a fairly crude policy instrument where a small change can have big effects at the school level. Because of the sensitivity of the formula to minor amendments and the pressures on LEAs to revise their formulae, schools are unlikely to enjoy a stable funding regime when transitional arrangements are over (Levačić, 1993). One of the side effects of formula funding and instability of funding will be that schools will build up bank balances e.g. Downes (1993).

Cost Containment and the Need to Reduce or Stabilise the Rate of Statementing

Cost containment refers to the objective of public expenditure control. An allocation system which provides additional resources to any pupil who can be certified or measured as meeting the criterion for additional resources provides an incentive for parents and the school to secure the necessary identification for that pupil. It can therefore be hypothesised that such an allocation system will over time generate increases in the number of pupils eligible for additional funding. I shall refer to this behaviour with respect to statements as 'statementing inflation' or 'resource drift' (Dessent, 1987). This development will over time either increase the total special educational needs budget by diverting resources from other areas of the education service, other services or by increased government grant or local taxation. If the additional expenditure on special educational needs is funded out of other sources than the education budget then it is not at the expense of other pupils. However there is no guarantee that this is the case, in which event statementing inflation has equity implications for the education service of which educationalists are not usually aware.

There is definite evidence that 'statementing inflation' does occur. The 1981 Education Act introduced procedures for the assessment and production of statements for pupils with special educational needs. The 1994 Code of Practice stated that:

> Only in a small minority of cases – nationally, around two per cent of children – will a child have special educational needs of a severity or complexity which requires the LEA to determine the LEA to determine and arrange the special educational provision for the child by means of a statutory statement of special educational needs (para. 2:1).

Since the implementation of the 1981 Education Act in 1983 there has been a general rise in the number of statements issued. Data obtained from the DfES statistics section for all 150 English LEAs indicates that there has been an overall increase in the percentage of statements from 1.6 per cent to 3.0 per cent during the period 1985 to 2002 (see also DfES, 2002c). The 1985 figures include some artificially low percentages due to the lateness of a few LEAs to issue transitional statements, e.g. five LEAs had records of 0.0 per cent. The explanation usually given for the increase is that it is partly, due to better identification and assessment procedures but, perhaps more importantly, due to parents and schools increasingly seeking statutory assessments in order to meet the needs of pupils with special educational needs.

Several writers have commented on the gross inequities which can occur when individualised provision is made by statements with children with similar levels of need receiving different levels of resource. Additionally there is the issue of the 'resource divide' described by Dessent (1987) whereby the continuum of need is resourced in a discontinuous way. Again the choice of purpose for SEN additional funding will help to determine the importance of this principle. It could be argued that compensatory resourcing should help to reduce the demand for statementing as in general terms the schools with the highest level of need as determined by a proxy indicator will receive higher levels of resources. However in practice, without LEA records to identify individual pupils experiencing SEN then 'double resourcing' often takes place, in which pupils with a statement also receive an allocation for FSM. In addition, without accountability, to be discussed in the next section, schools have not had to demonstrate their effectiveness with this additional funding and may not even be aware of the level of funding for this purpose within the formula.

Accountability

If the LEA is unsure about whether the purpose is for compensatory reasons or to raise school achievement then it is not surprising that schools show a lack of awareness about the amount of money that has been allocated by the formula to SEN. The Audit Commission (1992a) stated that:

> The key factor which is missing in considerations of the use of resources for pupils with special needs is an analysis of what funds are expected to achieve in terms of a child fulfilling his or her potential. (paragraph 113).

It continued (1992b):

> Accountability should go hand-in-hand with the delegation of funds to schools. Schools should be held responsible for the use of resources and for what they have achieved with them. Objective indicators in this area can be an incentive to schools to achieve well. (p.2).

It is significant to note that 60 per cent of headteachers were not aware of the special needs resources they did get in 1992. The Audit Commission/HMI report (1992a) considered that this situation arose because LEAs have not been sufficiently clear about amounts in schools' budgets which relate to special needs and partly because headteachers have not seen it as a priority to find this out (para.74).

There are further examples to illustrate schools' lack of awareness. Firstly, during a survey of pupils with special educational needs in mainstream schools, HMI (Ofsted, 1996) noted that:

> In the earlier stages of the survey, many schools had an inaccurate knowledge of the exact level of resourcing for pupils with SEN. Towards the end of the survey, schools became more aware of the delegated funding available for special educational needs, and this strengthened their monitoring of the provisions available (p6).

Secondly, a similar point about schools lack of awareness was raised by the House of Commons Education Committee regarding the working of the Code of Practice and the Special Needs Tribunal (House of Commons Education Committee, 1996). Mr Gerry Steinberg MP questioned Mr Vincent McDonnell (representing the Society of Education Officers):

> (Mr Steinberg) Are you actually saying that schools, under local management of schools, have money allocated to them from the local authority for special needs and have not actually spent it on special needs, they have spent it elsewhere?
> (Mr McDonnell) Potentially this has happened, yes.
> (Mr Steinberg) That is interesting. I think you are going to have to keep an eye on that, to be quite honest. (paras. 8, 9 and 11).

The degree to which LEAs can keep an eye on accountability is limited of course, due to the delegated powers given to governing bodies under LMS. However the main point to be remembered is that if LEAs specify the reason for additional resources, a proactive message will be delivered to schools and governing bodies about their intended use. In the light of these comments it is perhaps surprising to note that the arrangements adopted by *Whiteshire,* in response to appeals heard by the Special Educational Needs Tribunal, does not request evidence from the Headteacher as to how the school is spending the portion of its budget allocated by SEN indicators. The requirements of the 1993 Education Act states that the governing body must:

...do their best to secure that the necessary provision is made for any pupil who has special educational needs.

...report annually to parents on the school's policy for pupils with special educational needs (Section 161, DFE, 1994, p6).

Some governing bodies have interpreted this to include in the annual report to parents, details of the use of SEN resources, the total expenditure and an evaluation.

It is likely that a higher profile will continually be given by LEAs to the accountability of non-statemented special educational needs resources particularly in the light of reports from LEAs which appear to show that schools are carrying forward significant underspends into the following financial year (see Downes, 1993). It should also be borne in mind that there are inherent costs involved in rendering accountability e.g. paper production and checking. Therefore the most efficient form of accountability needs consideration.

Bines and Loxley (1995) have argued that the Code of Practice for Special Educational Needs will also increase accountability in relation to provision and partnership with parents. In general allocation systems, based on differentiated indicators of individual pupils' special needs which specify the expected educational achievement, lend themselves much more readily to accountability for the effectiveness with which resources have been used.

Summary

This Chapter has taken a technical perspective in outlining the general principles against which the provision of additional resources for special educational needs can be evaluated. However the application of explicit normative criteria does not, of course, give unequivocal guidance to budget construction (Levačić, 1989). Additionally I shall consider in Chapter Seven how the policy discourses of the 'special needs pupil' and the 'school and teacher effectiveness' are accommodated within this 'rational' framework.

The principles may be mutually inconsistent and so it is important to consider their relative effects. For example, the construction of a complex formula which places emphasis on the concept of equity may make the whole process less accountable and would fail the 'simplicity rule'. At an individual school level, the consequences of formula funding depend not merely on the design of the formula, which is essentially a static concept, but also on the nature of the school's market where choices made by parents and other factors influence the size and composition of the pupil's population (Simkins, 1995). The distribution of resources within a market model will change over time and will depend on the quality of resources a school can attract (e.g. teacher experience and qualifications) and the characteristics of the pupil population, particularly if consideration is taken of Monk's (1990) evidence about peer group effects on achievement.

A clear set of general principles for providing additional resources formula funding can assist the partnership between LEAs, governing bodies and headteachers (Association of Metropolitan Authorities, 1995). More and more pressure is being put upon governing bodies to divert monies to other areas from budgets which have been originally allocated by LEAs for non-statemented SEN. Without accountability of these in-house resources, there is evidence that referrals for statutory assessment will increase to gain access to further funding from the LEA. The implications of an increasing statutory assessment component of the LEA budget will have a direct influence on the amount of money which is left for calculating the age weighted pupil units and the non-statemented SEN allocation (see Audit Commission, 2002). Increasing the non-statemented SEN allocation and developing a SEN formula which includes differentiation of funding levels will not by itself reduce the continuing trend in the increase of statements. LEAs are attempting to develop robust and transparent SEN policies which clearly define the threshold of need to trigger a statutory assessment and documents the LEAs' expectation of schools' responsibilities (Coopers and Lybrand, 1996a). If LEAs are successful in controlling and stabilising the costs involved with the increase in the number of pupils with statements, then this may offer the possibility for some recycling of resources to the non-statemented sector. In addition an understanding of the issues and general principles of formula funding will enable LEAs to adjust and review their own formula to reflect policies and objectives.

Chapter 4

Historic Funding of Special Educational Needs and the Relationship with Formula Funding

The second subsidiary aim of this book is to examine the funding relationship for non-statemented special educational needs and pupils with statements in an attempt to develop a coherent approach to resourcing throughout the continuum of SEN. The purpose of this Chapter is to concentrate on the fourth Key Question i.e. to draw out the historic association between special educational needs with provision and funding by consideration of a literature search and reference to the pertinent government circulars of guidance.

The first section of this Chapter will examine the relationship between special needs and resources as illustrated by two important circulars of their time i.e. Circular 4/73, (DES 1973) and Circular 11/90 (DES, 1990). Although both of these circulars relate to the 'two per cent' of pupils with SEN, it is important to be aware of the government's recommendations for resource levels in the context of the continuum of SEN. Circular 4/73 provided guidance to LEAs on staffing ratios in special schools and classes, using categories of handicap and maximum class sizes. The general issue of class size in mainstream schools will then be discussed, which has gained in importance over recent years. Class size is particularly crucial when determining resource levels for pupils on a per capita basis, where each pupil is funded for a fraction of a teacher, as recommended by the LMS proposals. Circular 11/90 provided an update of 4/73 and proposed the concept of resource bands based on five bands of learning difficulty.

The second part of the Chapter will examine the impact of LMS/Fair Funding on the formula funding arrangements for special educational needs. There are three major functions of a funding formula (Ross and Levačić, 1999) : a market regulation function, an equity function and a directive function. The market regulation function has been predominant during the period 1988 to 1997 during which time the Conservative government was in power. There was an assumption by the government that parents would choose schools on the basis of the quality of the education provided and an important element to influence choice would be to improve the level of school output information available to parents. In this way as resources would follow the pupil, so 'good' school would prosper and 'poor' schools would either improve or leave the market place. The second major function of a funding formula is concerned with equity and this is of particular importance when determining resource levels for pupils with special educational needs, the main focus of this book. The directive function of the formula is an important instrument by which the LEA can implement policies using financial incentives e.g. by protecting the size of small schools or by encouraging the specific use of resources e.g. for the teaching of English as a second language to pupils from an ethnic minority background. It will be argued later in this book (Chapter Seven) that the part of the formula concerned with funding for non-statemented special educational needs should encompass both the equity and directive functions.

Pupil Teacher Ratios And Class Size

An essential concept in the understanding of resource issues for pupils with special educational needs is how the amount of resource or the 'fraction of a teacher' is calculated. This section will discuss four resourcing areas relating to pupil teacher ratios and class size. First, Circular 4/73 will be examined which provided guidance for LEAs on staffing in special schools based on pupil-teacher ratios; second, the concept of curriculum based staffing will be discussed, which emerged because of concerns about the teacher-pupil ratio; third, activity led staffing which was developed from the curriculum led approach and fourth, a brief literature review on class size will be provided.

DES Circular 4/73

The relationship between needs and resources is illustrated in Circular 4/73 (DES, 1973) which provided guidance for LEAs on staffing in special schools and classes using the categories of handicap and maximum class sizes. This circular replaced the regulations issued in 1959 when maximum class sizes in special schools were prescribed by the Handicapped Pupils and Special Schools Regulations (Regulation 9) (Ministry of Education, 1959a), (see Table 4.1).

Table 4.1   Staffing recommendations for children with special educational needs taken from Ministry of Education (1959a) and DES Circular 4/73

Category of Handicap	Prescribed Maximum Class Size 1959	Recommended Teaching Group Size 1973
Deaf/Partially Hearing	10	6-8
Speech Defects	10	6-8
Blind	15	6
Partially Sighted	15	9
Maladjusted	15	7
Educationally Sub-normal Moderate ESN(M)	20	11-13
Educationally Sub-normal Severe ESN(S)	N/A	10
Epileptic	20	8-10
Physically Handicapped	20	4/5-10
Delicate	30	4/5-10
Autistic	Not given	6-8

Note: ESN(S) children were termed 'unsuitable for education in school' until the 1970 Education (Handicapped Children) Act transferred the responsibility from the health to the education authorities.

Circular 4/73 indicated that:

The increased complexity of the disabilities found among children, and improvements in the supply of teachers since the regulations were made, have resulted in average class sizes well below the prescribed maxima for a number of handicaps. Thus, in January 1970 the average class sizes in special schools for the blind, the maladjusted and the physically handicapped were 9.2, 9.0 and 12.6 respectively, against the maxima prescribed by regulations of 15, 15 and 20. For other handicaps, notably the educationally sub-normal, average class sizes were closer to the prescribed maxima (para. 3).

Three important principles were encompassed by Circular 4/73. Firstly, the rigid concept of class size was replaced by the principle of pupil teacher ratios (PTR) which allowed flexibility to be built into the organisation of the work of each school. Thus flexible teaching groups were envisaged ranging from individual tuition to groups of 20 or more for music and games. The second principle was that the more severe the learning handicap, the smaller should be the teaching group, recognising that children with multiple handicaps make the greatest demands of all. Thirdly, it was felt that with young children a more favourable staffing ratio was required.

Curriculum Based Staffing

Despite the adoption of the principle of PTRs in Circular 4/73 there were concerns about the shortcomings of their use. The White Paper of 1972 *Education : A Framework for Expansion* indicated that:

> It (PTR) does not allow for changes in the age distribution of the school population. For example, an increase, within a given school population, in the proportion of older pupils with their more favourable staffing ratio would necessitate an improvement in the overall ratio merely to retain the same standards.

According to Simpson (1987) the concept of curriculum based or curriculum related staffing (CBS/CRS) '*was born of dissatisfactions with the pupil-teacher ratio*'. Under this traditional approach of PTR schools were entitled to a teacher for every set number of pupils they enrolled and the number of teachers per pupil varied according to the age of the pupils concerned. The value of the curriculum-led approach was that it focused on the impact of the curriculum and class sizes on the staffing requirements of each school and did not simply rely on the application of pupil-teacher ratios to arrive at the staffing complement of each school. However it was not until the contraction in the education system, evidenced by falling pupil rolls, became a reality in the 1980s that alternatives to the PTR were taken seriously.

The basis of the curriculum-led approach was the adoption of a curriculum model which laid out for each of the first five years of secondary education, the distribution of the 40-period week between various subjects or groups of subjects. This was then used to calculate the number of teachers required to teach the curriculum once the average class sizes had been decided upon, together with the range of choice of subjects to be offered in later years. The CBS/CRS policies were also not without critics as is shown by the comments from a Headteacher from *Whiteshire,* an LEA used in the case study referred to in detail in Chapter Six.

> ... the CRS policy so called which wasn't really a CRS policy at all. It was just a group size policy, under which you got a number of teachers delivered by various group sizes 16, 19, 24 and all those various numbers that are floating around the system. At the end of the day if that and a bit of small school supplement didn't get you to 18.5 to 1 then you were given 18.5 to 1 anyway. (Headteacher)

Activity Led Staffing

Activity Led Staffing (ALS) was developed from the curriculum-led approach in the late 1980s with the introduction of Local Management of Schools. It extended the analysis further and included, as well as class teaching, all the other activities that teachers undertake. The rationale of ALS has been described as establishing a benchmark for resources which is related realistically to the nature and scale of activity in schools (Cambridgeshire County Council, 1993). The main aim of ALS then is to identify the curriculum and management's activities within schools and to quantify the resources required to carry out these activities. This approach is seen as particularly important in assessing the resources required when new demands are placed on schools such as the introduction of the National Curriculum and assessment, records of achievement, teacher appraisal, Ofsted inspections or the costs of implementing the Code of Practice on the identification and assessment of special educational needs.

A number of steps are required to arrive at an ALS system of funding (Cambridgeshire County Council, 1993). Defining the activities undertaken by teachers is the crucial first stage in ALS. The stages are:

- Design stage – this involves identifying all the curriculum and management activities carried out in schools;
- Parameter values are inserted – these drive the model and consist of the numbers or standards (parameters) which will set against curriculum and management activities which constitute the model;
- Calculations take place to determine the number of teachers required to deliver the model on the basis of the parameters decided on in the stage above;
- Actual cost of employing teachers is calculated.

A particular problem that LEAs have found is that ALS models tend to generate budgets that are often far in excess of their Education Standard Spending Assessments. In Hampshire a working party proposed an activity-led staffing model which, if translated into funding, would have required a 50 per cent increase in the funding of primary school staffing. A subsequent report from Hampshire County Council pointed out that 'such increases in funding will not be possible without changes in national policies and budgets'. The issue of underfunding as defined by ALS models has meant that LEAs have had to make a difficult choice, either to alter the ALS parameters until they offer the 'best fit' to the available resources or to abandon the ALS approach at least temporarily. In Cambridgeshire, for example, the parameters were adjusted to meet the available expenditure by using relative weights for different age groups, whilst in Leeds LEA it was decided that it would not be fair to implement a sub-optimal scheme and it was recommended that further work should be undertaken to develop a model that was fair at low resource levels.

The next section will provide a brief look at the research on class size, an area which has a significant impact on ALS and resourcing for pupils with special educational needs but without statements. The White Paper *Excellence in schools* (DfEE, 1997a) outlined the government's intention to reduce class sizes for 5, 6 and 7 year olds to 30 or below by 2002.

Literature Review on Class Size

Class sizes have been long regarded as an central factor within education e.g. Bennett, 1996. Although there is a wide spread belief amongst parents, teachers and others that pupils learn most effectively in small classes, the research evidence according to the Director of the National Foundation for Educational Research, 'has been conflicting, inconclusive and disappointingly meagre' (Burstall, 1992).

The literature on class size has been reviewed by Mortimore and Blatchford (1993) and Blatchford and Mortimore (1994). They concluded that there is now firm evidence of a link between class size and educational attainment but only in the early years, especially with disadvantaged pupils and only with classes smaller than 20. Research was quoted from the USA from the so called STAR project (which stands for 'student-teacher achievement ratio'). This is a major state-wide intervention in Tennessee which included over 7,000 pupils in 79 schools. It compared pupils in three types of classes:

1. 'small' classes (13-17)
2. 'regular' classes (22-25)
3. 'regular' with full-time teacher aide.

Pupils were followed through from kindergarten (aged 5) in 1985 to third grade (aged 8) in 1989. Pupils were then (and are still being) followed, after the experimental stage, into grades 4-6, and beyond in the Lasting Benefits Study (LBS). Based on the STAR results, a new initiative was begun in Tennessee by providing incentives in 17 counties to reduce class size to 1:15 in grades K-3 (see Nye et al. 1993).

Nye et al. (1992) reported that the results were impressive and consistent. In both reading and mathematics pupils in small classes performed significantly better than pupils in regular classes. This was true from Kindergarten to grade 3. Interestingly, being in regular class with a teacher aide made no difference; small classes with one qualified teacher had pupils who did better than pupils in regular classes with an assistant; and there appeared to be a particular advantage for pupils from ethnic minorities. The gains still appeared to be evident when the pupils returned to regular classes. The Lasting Benefits Study (Nye et al. 1992) found that significant differences were still evident for the two school years after returning to regular classes, that is grades 4 and 5. Even though the authors agreed with the view that the their research is the 'most significant research in the USA in the last 25 years' there is still need for caution. Although Slavin (1989) agrees that substantial reductions in class size do have positive effects, the size of the difference reported in even good quality research studies is moderate. He reviewed eight studies of primary aged children, including the STAR research, which met three selection criteria. Firstly, comparisons between small and large classes over a period of one year; secondly, comparisons of larger classes with classes at least 30 per cent smaller and containing no more than 20 pupils and thirdly, using random assignment or matching with initial equivalence. However, the sizes of the effects for the STAR research are more marked than most of the figures cited by Slavin. It seems reasonable to conclude that the most thorough research, which would be expected to result in the most reliable evidence, has produced the most marked effects, (Blatchford and Mortimore, 1994).

Blatchford and Mortimore have also considered the particular concerns about class size reductions. Firstly, class size reductions would appear to be more effective in the first years of school, when children are more dependent on adult help. Achilles et al. (1993) claim that for benefits to result, pupils have to start school in small classes; entering small classes later has less benefit for pupils and cannot be expected on its own to affect difficulties that may have developed. The second main concern with class size reductions is the expenditure. It has been estimated that after seven years the Prime Time project in Indiana has cost $82 million (Weis, 1990). Tomlinson (1990) has questioned whether this expenditure is justified given the lack of evidence of clear effects. Blatchford and Mortimore (1994) give the example from one LEA that to reduce all classes by one pupil would cost approximately £1 million. To reduce classes from 30 to 20 pupils would be seen by education officers and elected members to be too expensive and would be construed to be better spent in other ways e.g. to increase primary non-class contact time.

A third question about class reductions is how much they have to be reduced in order to be effective. The consensus from the American research according to Blatchford and Mortimore, seems to be that reducing class size by a few pupils across the board is unlikely to be effective and that significant effects will not be achieved until classes are reduced to below 20. This evidence does not necessarily produce beneficial effects in all aspects of education. Shapson et al. (1980) found that teachers do not change their methods and styles of teaching when faced with fewer students. Their research discovered that teachers had firm expectations about the positive effects of class size but these consistently failed to match what was observed in the classroom. The concern might be that class sizes could make teachers feel more comfortable and make their lives easier without necessarily improving the quality of teaching or the curriculum experienced by the pupils.

A number of commentators have advocated the need for new research on class size in the UK e.g. Bassey (1995), Mortimore and Blatchford (1995), and Bennett (1996), despite the assertion by Hodgetts (1995) that the argument is not really about class size at all but about the political decision of how much of the public expenditure budget should be allocated to education. The argument has been proffered by researchers in education that, given the basic importance of class size and how it determines vast costs in education, it is surprising how little investment has been put into research on class sizes and teaching groups, on the effects on teachers and pupils of different class sizes, and on the opportunities that might be provided.

In summary although the research evidence on the benefits of smaller classes is not clear cut, it does appear that pupils educated in smaller classes during the early years of schooling out-perform pupils in larger classes and maintain their advantage, demonstrating increased attainment two years later. Children from disadvantaged backgrounds appear to benefit most. This finding has implications for LEA policy makers, for example Staffordshire LEA (1995) proposed to direct additional funds to the most disadvantaged schools at Key Stage 1. However it is important to remember that real improvements to pupil attainments depend on a combination of factors and not simply class size. This is emphasised by the research concerned with investigating teacher, school and other effects on pupil achievement e.g. Rutter et al. (1979) and Mortimore et al. (1988). The evidence suggests that factors such as classroom management, classroom interactions and climate, and the peer group (home environment/parental support) are much more significant than simply per-pupil expenditure.

Staffing for Pupils with Special Educational Needs – The Concept of Resource Bands of Learning Difficulty (DES Circular 11/90)

DES Circular 11/90 (DES, 1990) outlined the considerations which LEAs and schools should bear in mind when determining staffing levels for pupils with statements of special educational needs. In practice staffing for pupils with SEN typically includes the involvement of both teachers and classroom ancillaries which were referred to in the Circular as special support assistants. It set out a possible model (see Table 4.2) in five bands of learning difficulty to assess the staff time needed per pupil, in terms of teacher and special support assistants or teacher assistants to take account of the particular learning difficulties of each child. The Circular stated that:

> The model derives from observations of classroom work seen to promote effective learning and care for various groups of pupils... The model proposes that one means of assessing pupils' SEN is in terms of the demands made upon the teachers and the extent to which teaching methods have to be adapted to meet those demands. The model is soundly based on good practice. By relating the complexity of pupils' learning difficulties to his or her needs for a balanced and broadly based curriculum, judgements can be made about the likely levels of demand made upon teachers and Special Support Assistants. This complexity is reflected in the bands of learning difficulty described in Annex A (i.e. Table 4.2) (para. 6).

The Circular also stressed the point that the model should only be taken as a starting point for assessing staffing levels and that they should not be taken as indicating staffing minima to be applied in all cases. As Norgate (1995) suggests ultimately the LEA will need to be sensitive to local circumstances rather than to use the circular to justify minimum levels of staffing.

**Table 4.2   A Staffing Model as described in DES Circular 11/90
             Annex A**

Band of Learning Difficulty	Primary		Secondary	
	Teacher per pupil	Special Support Assistant/ Teaching Assistant per pupil	Teacher per pupil	Special Support Assistant/ Teaching Assistant per pupil
1. Profound and multiple learning difficulties	0.2	0.3*	0.2	0.3*
2. Severe communication difficulties	0.18	0.18	0.18	0.10
3. Severe emotional and behavioural difficulties	0.15	0.15	0.15	0.15
4. Severe developmental difficulties	0.13	0.13	0.13	0.13
5. Other learning difficulties	0.1	0.1	0.1	0.05

* In a group of 10 pupils the maximum number of Special Support Assistants will be 3.

Circular 11/90 concluded with this caution about the difficulty in providing definitive guidance and warns against an over-simplistic application of this model.

There can be no blueprint for ideal staffing arrangements in any institution making provision for pupils with SEN since much will depend upon the particular circumstances of that institution, the mix of skills of its teaching and non-teaching staff, and the nature of the needs of its pupils, both as individuals and as a group. ...The Secretary of State offers the advice in this Circular as a contribution to LEAs and governors' own consideration and planning to that end (para. 25).

Interestingly, the principle adopted in Circular 4/73, that young children require a more favourable staffing ratio was not supported by the model of staffing proposed in Circular 11/90. The reasons for this are given in Touche Ross (1990):

*   whilst the age of a pupil in a mainstream school generally provides some indication of the learning stage reached by the child, pupils with special needs may well progress at unpredictable rates, and knowledge of their ages provides no such indication;
*   some pupils require substantial care or medical support throughout their school career, and the cost of this support remains broadly constant whatever their age.

As Touche Ross continue, that is not to say there are not significant differences between the funding requirements of schools catering for dissimilar age-groups. For example, there was general agreement that:

*   the youngest pupils in special schools (who are sometimes much younger than mainstream pupils) would need significant extra carer and supervision;
*   in their final years of schooling pupils should be prepared for life in the outside world, perhaps through work or college placements, or through taking public examinations.

The Touche Ross report concluded that a formula based on age-weighted pupil units would be inappropriate for special schools, as originally Circular 7/88 envisaged. It suggested that the differences between the needs of school populations may be better recognised by considering the overall age group of the school rather than the ages of the individual pupils. The suggestions of the Touche Ross report were incorporated into Circular 7/91 which will be discussed in the next section.

Importantly, there was no mention in both Circulars 4/73 and 11/90 of any objective basis for calculating the staffing ratios e.g. Norgate, 1995. The final sentence of the Circular 4/73 read:

The Secretary of State believes that the flexibility encouraged as a result in staffing arrangements should make it possible to match special school provision even more closely than before to the widely varying needs of handicapped children.

Circular 11/90 states that the model:

> ...derives from observations of classroom work seen to promote learning and care for various groups of pupils (para. 6).

The use of the concepts of 'need' and 'learning and care' neatly side-steps the fundamental issues of 'resourceworthiness' and degree of need. Dessent (1987) points to the issues as being essentially ethical in nature as any discussion of special education is unavoidably a discussion concerning questions of value and ethics in terms of the distribution of society's educational resources. The issue of whether it is worthwhile to provide differential resourcing levels will be addressed in Chapter Seven.

Local Management of Schools and Fair Funding

The 1988 Education Act has been described as the most important piece of educational legislation in the United Kingdom since 1944. Local Management of Schools (LMS), was a key policy of this Act and has brought radical changes to the way schools are run and how resources are allocated both within mainstream and special schools. In April 1999 LMS was replaced by a new framework called Fair Funding following the passage of the 1998 Standards and Framework Act. This section will look at LMS in greater detail before describing the Fair Funding arrangements.

Underpinning the statutory detail of LMS are two fundamental principles:

- allocating resources to schools on an equitable basis, and
- giving schools considerably greater autonomy in the management of those resources.
  (para.1 Circular 2/94).

A number of commentators have described the trend of decentralisation as a growing feature of the school systems throughout the western world (e.g. Hill et al., 1990). The rationale behind this trend is the observation that there has been a considerable growth in centralised administration. Several national governments and their agencies have come to the view that too many decisions were located at a distance from the place of learning. This has led to initiatives taking place and later national policies and guidelines being formulated in the Netherlands, the USA, Australia, New

Zealand, England and Wales. As Lowe Boyd (1992) notes, despite differences in political and social context, there are striking parallels in contemporary educational reforms adopted by English-speaking countries, in particular Australia, New Zealand, the UK and the USA. These countries have combined both decentralisation of management decision-making to schools and a tendency to stronger centralisation of control over specifying and monitoring educational standards. Levačić (1995) feels that recent developments in these directions in continental Europe seem to be less marked, although Spain, the Netherlands and Finland were singled out by the OECD (1992) as having the highest proportion of decisions taken at school level (between 45 and 56 per cent).

The general aim of these educational reforms has been to introduce a more competitive market approach to the allocation of resources in the education system. Chapter Three has already outlined the political thinking of the new Right which evolved during the late 1970s and 1980s. This promoted the view that children's education is a consumer good to be obtained through parental choice. Allied to this is the assumption that market forces will ensure parents get what they demand, as these changes will move inevitably in the direction of rising standards (Wallace, 1993). However education cannot be a 'market' in the strict sense because it is a public utility, therefore the term quasi-markets has been used by Le Grand and Bartlett (1993), which they acknowledge to Williamson (1975, p.8). Quasi-markets are 'markets' because they replace administrative allocation of resources by the separation of purchasers and providers and instil a degree of competition between providers for clients. The quasi-market remains highly regulated. The government continues to control such matters as the quality of service (as with the national curriculum) and price, which is often set to zero to the user, as in schooling. In this way the markets are 'quasi' because they differ from conventional markets in a number of other ways. There are differences both on both the supply and the demand side. On the supply side as with conventional markets, there is competition between productive enterprises or service suppliers. Thus taking the context of education, the schools are seen to compete for customers, their pupils. However schools are not out to maximise their profits, nor are they privately owned. On the demand side, prices are regulated or set to zero, so for example consumer purchasing power is not expressed in money terms in quasi-markets. Instead either it takes the form of an earmarked budget or 'voucher' confined to the purchase of a specific service allocated to others, or it is centralised in a state purchasing agency, the LEA. Thirdly, in most cases it is not the direct user who exercises the choices concerning purchasing decisions. Instead these choices are often delegated to a third party such as parents who can exercise choice of school thereby determining a large component of the school budget by the number of pupils that are enrolled. However school places would still be rationed and total numbers would be determined by a state agency such as the LEA.

A key part of the quasi-market is the use of formula funding to allocate resources directly to schools. The previous Chapter has already noted that the Plowden Report (CACE, 1967) encouraged LEAs to develop policies of positive discrimination in the distribution of educational resources which included the use of formula or educational priority indices.

Formula Funding was proposed by Local Management of Schools as an alternative method of resource allocation to the three main systems of historic funding, bidding and officer discretion described by Knight (1993a). Section 38 (1) of the 1988 Education Act required each LEA to determine a 'formula' for allocating a share of the Aggregated Schools Budget (ASB) to each of the schools covered in its scheme. Under Section 38 the formula:

- may include 'methods, principles and rules of any description, however expressed' (Section 38(2)). The formula does not have to be expressed in purely algebraic form, but it must apply a consistent set of criteria for distributing resources;
- may include 'provision for taking into account any other factors affecting the needs of individual schools which are subject to variation from school to school'. The formula can take account of relevant factors other than age-weighted pupil numbers, including in particular 'the number of registered pupils at a school who have special educational needs and the nature of the special educational provision made for them' (Section 38(3)(b)).

Devising an acceptable formula for pupils with non-statemented special educational needs has been one of the most difficult tasks for LEAs. The task has become all the more arduous as serious tensions exist between the 1981 Education Act and the 1988 Education Reform Act (Wedell, 1988). The definition of special educational needs in the 1981 Act marked a change from a 'within child' view to an 'interactive' view. In other words special educational needs are the outcome of the interaction between the resources and deficiencies within a child and the resources and deficiencies within the environment (Goacher et al., 1988). A main tenet of LMS is the emphasis on the individual pupil as the main unit of resource which sits uncomfortably with the 'interactive' view of special educational needs.

The first generation of LMS SEN formulae saw the majority of LEAs using free school meals (FSM) data obtained at the school level, to solve the problem of predicting the incidence of SEN. Despite LEAs expressing their unease with using FSM, there has been an increase in use from 81 per cent to 96 per cent over the ten year period 1992-2002 (Marsh, 2002). The EMIE survey also noted that LEAs are using more direct or 'needs' related measures in conjunction with deprivation indicators e.g. the use of professional audits and the use of test results. This change in thinking by LEAs is in line with the Code of Practice which has encouraged the cult of individualism. The rhetoric of individual education plans and individual needs is evidence of Hargreaves' (1982) argument that schools have become so involved with the rights, progress and the welfare of the individual pupil that they have lost sight of the corporate aspects of school life. Therefore the tension exists in the context of formula design whether it is sufficient to predict the incidence of SEN, which could be achieved by the use of FSM data, or whether the emphasis should be on the identification of individual SEN as recommended by the Code of Practice. A main implication of the different approaches is that the use of FSM implies a less specific demonstration of accountability of funds than the use of individual pupil measures of special educational needs.

The case for using formula funding relies on the assumption that the formula is well designed and is not merely the product of whatever LEA wide data was available at the time of the LMS/Fair Funding scheme being forwarded to the Department for Education and Skills for approval. The main asset of a formula is that it is objective and transparent and can be a highly visible piece of policy implementation.

As stated earlier in this section, Fair Funding has now replaced LMS. The new arrangements required LEAs to delegate all funding to schools except where it corresponds to LEA responsibilities of non school activities, strategic management, access, school improvement and special educational needs. The government have gradually increased the target for delegation and at 2002-03 this was set at 87 per cent of the Local Schools Budget. Starting in 1999, the new arrangements were phased in over two years and encompassed all schools including the ex grant maintained schools which were abolished. The Audit Commission estimated that the amount delegated to schools in England and Wales increased by over £600 million as a result of 'Fair Funding' (Audit Commission, (2000).

There are certain budget restrictions regarding the amount which can be delegated which relate to the structure of the non-statemented SEN formula. A formula requirement is that 80 per cent of the total amount available for primary and secondary schools must be allocated on the basis of pupil numbers (known as pupil led funding) or age weighted pupil units (AWPUs). This has been reduced to 75 per cent for 2002/03. However, the definition of 'pupil-led' includes any funding delegated for pupils with statements (even when allocated on a basis not directly linked to pupil numbers), and can also include funding - amounting to up to 5 per cent of the primary and secondary share of the Individual Schools Budget - for pupils with SEN but without statements. This latter amount is sometimes known as the 'hidden 5 per cent' because many LEAs have not made it clear in their budget statements that this money exists or have not defined its purpose. In addition to the 5 per cent, LEAs may also allocate further sums of money within the 'other' or non-pupil led part of the formula. Chapter Five shows that the expenditure in LEAs on additional and special educational needs (AEN/SEN) ranges from £8 per pupil to £270 per pupil. The next Chapter will also illustrate the indicators which LEAs are currently using to assess the numbers of pupils with AEN/SEN.

Summary

This Chapter has looked at the relationship of special educational needs with historical funding arrangements, in particular with the policy of formula funding arrangements as introduced by Local Management of Schools (LMS and now replaced by Fair Funding. The three major functions of formula funding have been highlighted i.e. market regulation, equity and the directive function and it has been shown that formula funding can be a key instrument of policy if well designed.

Although there appears to be general support for the decentralisation of managerial decision making to the school level, a number of commentators have expressed concerns about the serious tensions which exist when the use of market philosophy is applied to the area of special educational needs e.g. Evans and Lunt (1990); Vincent et al. (1994) and Housden (1992) who have all argued that the overall impact of LMS on LEA's approach to SEN is likely to be negative.

> ...a market-oriented discourse, within a quasi-market framework, encourages an emphasis on individualism which is antithetical to the concept of a planned and pervasive approach to provision for 'vulnerable children' (Housden, 1992).

This is an example of the tension between the two policy discourses of the 'special needs pupil' and 'school and teacher effectiveness'.

The complex task of identification and description of children's needs within the formula should, in theory, take account of the relative and interactive nature of special educational needs which lie along a continuum from greater to lesser need. In other words the 'school and teacher effectiveness' discourse should be accommodated, however in the context of formula funding it is difficult to see how this can be included. In other words there is the danger that formula funding will drive LEAs further towards the discourse of the special needs pupil without a full appreciation of other possible discourses of the conceptualisation of special educational needs. Whilst this concern is real it is important to remember that there was no golden age of SEN resourcing in the days before LMS and that the benefits of formula funding, which encompass the principles of objectivity, effectiveness, equity and transparency, were all missing when education officer discretion was the funding method of choice for LEAs.

Chapter 5

Funding Methods used by Local Education Authorities to Determine Special Educational Needs

The first part of this book has provided an analysis and discussion of the underlying issues surrounding the conceptualisation of needs within the framework of Local Management of Schools (LMS) and the Code of Practice. It has shown that the policy thrust has been on the identification and assessment of the individual child's difficulties and has reinforced the special needs discourse rather than consideration of wider issues such as those portrayed by the 'school and teacher effectiveness' discourse.

This Chapter continues with the second subsidiary aim of the book namely the examination of the funding relationship between non-statemented special educational needs and pupils with statements to develop a coherent approach to resourcing throughout the continuum of SEN. To this end Key Question 5 will be held up to scrutiny i.e. what is the current practice in LEAs with regard to resource definition, resource allocation and resource management? The Chapter will also consider whether the various principles for evaluating a funding formula, mentioned in Chapter Three, are better delivered by some types of SEN allocation system than by others.

The results of a national survey will be analysed which illustrates the methods adopted by Local Education Authorities (LEAs), in their attempts to find solutions to the funding questions posed by the limitations of the government's legislation. The survey explores current practice in LEAs for resourcing additional and special educational needs in 2001/02. It was published by Education Management Information Exchange (EMIE) (Marsh, 2002) and was available to all LEAs in England, Wales, Scotland and Northern Ireland. The umbrella term 'additional and special educational needs' has been used throughout the survey and refers to a wide range of factors, relating to special educational needs and social deprivation, which LEAs take into account when funding schools.

Background to the Additional and Special Educational Needs Survey

The survey set out to analyse the additional and special educational needs of LEAs in England. During autumn 2001 all LEAs in England were invited to participate in the survey. Of the 150 LEAs in England, 107 (71 per cent) responded to the invitation to participate in the survey by submitting Table 3 from their 2001/02 Section 52 Budget Statement and other information about funding methods. The survey draws on the findings of two previous surveys: Lee (1992a) and Marsh (1997a) to enable comparisons to be made about the funding arrangements for pupils with additional and special educational needs over a ten-year period. The findings of the survey provided supplementary data to the DfES guidance to LEAs on *The Distribution of Resources to Support Inclusion* (DfES, 2001b) (also see Beek, 2002), the NFER study on Fair Funding (Evans et al., 2001) and the work of the DfES Education Strategy Funding Group. Previous surveys have been performed by NFER in 1994 reported in Fletcher-Campbell (1996), Robertson (1995), Coopers and Lybrand in 1995 reported in Coopers and Lybrand (1996a) and Bibby and Lunt (1996) using 1994/95 Budget Statements.

The survey will provide an update and overview of current practice by LEAs for resourcing additional and special educational needs (AEN/SEN) and will be structured around the following questions:

1. How do LEAs assess the numbers of pupils with additional and special educational needs?
2. How much extra resources are given by LEAs to pupils with additional and special educational needs?
3. What options are available for the distribution of the extra resources?

How do Local Education Authorities Assess the Numbers of Pupils with Additional and Special Educational Needs?

Further details of individual LEA AEN funding arrangements are to be found in Marsh, (2002). Table 5.1 shows that during the period 1992-2002 there has been a trend for LEAs to use more indicators to distribute resources for AEN/SEN. Two or more indicators are now used by 83 per cent of LEAs, which compares to 72 per cent in 1997 and 55 per cent in 1992.

Table 5.1   The percentage of LEAs using different numbers of indicators to fund AEN/SEN

No of Different Indicators	2002 n=107	1997 n=85	1992 n=72
0	0%	1%	3%
1	17%	27%	42%
2	30%	33%	28%
3	21%	19%	18%
4	21%	13%	7%
5	8%	5%	1%
6	3%	2%	1%
7	0%	-	-
8	1%	-	-

The DfES guidance *The Distribution of Resources to Support Inclusion*, gives details of three broad approaches to the distribution of resources for AEN/SEN i.e. indicators, direct pupil audit and allocation through groups of schools. The most widely used approach to resource allocation is by indicators and all LEAs in the survey now use at least one indicator. All of the LEAs using the direct pupil audit approach (16 per cent) combine this with at least one other indicator. Two LEAs allocate resources for exceptional needs through groups or clusters of schools and use FSM as a proxy indicator of AEN/SEN. Beek (2002) mentions that a number of other LEAs are also considering the distribution of resources through cluster or group arrangements.

Table 5.2 provides evidence about the indicators used by LEAs and whether there have been policy changes over the 10 year period 1992-2002. For the purposes of comparison, the broad distribution approach of direct pupil audit has been included in Table 5.2 as an indicator of AEN/SEN. Table 5.2 shows that FSM is still the most commonly used indicator, either individually or in combination with other factors. There has been an increase in the use of FSM from 81 per cent to 96 per cent over the ten-year period 1992-2002. This is a slightly surprising finding, as a number of LEAs are reported to be searching for alternatives to the use of free school meals, e.g. Dorset, Durham and Oxfordshire. Only two LEAs so far are making use of the Indices of Deprivation (IoD) although another two LEAs stated they were to make the change to IoD from free school meals in 2002-03. (See Office of the Deputy Prime Minister [formerly DTLR] website.)

Table 5.2 Percentage of LEAs using Indicators of AEN/SEN: comparisons with previous surveys (Lee, 1992a and Marsh, 1997a)

Indicators	2002	1997	1992
Free School Meals	96%	92%	81%
National Curriculum Assessments	31%	7%	-
Tests	27%	31%	28%
English as an Additional Language	25%	24%	29%
Mobility or Pupil Turnover	21%	31%	18%
Number on Roll	20%	6%	-
Audit	16%	8%	7%
Stage of Code of Practice	14%	14%	-
Baseline Assessment	11%	-	-
Education Welfare Benefits/Clothing Grants	5%	8%	14%
Index of Local Deprivation	2%	-	-
Other	16%	20%	-

The next three most used indicators are National Curriculum Assessments (NCA) or Standard Assessment Tests/Tasks (SATs) (31 per cent of LEAs), an increase from 7 per cent in 1997, standardised educational tests (27 per cent) and English as an additional language (EAL) (25 per cent). LEAs have also increased their use of the following indicators: number on roll (NOR) (0 per cent in 1992 to 20 per cent in 2002), direct pupil audit (7 per cent in 1992 to 16 per cent in 2002) and baseline assessment (0 per cent in 1992 to 11 per cent in 2002). The use of education welfare benefits is the only indicator to have declined over the ten-year period from 14 per cent in 1992 to 5 per cent in 2002.

How Much Extra Resources are Given by LEAs to Pupils with Additional Educational Needs?

There are three main levels of resourcing for pupils with additional and special educational needs. The first level is the Age Weighted Pupil Unit (AWPU) which forms a significant proportion of the mainstream schools' delegated budget. The second is specific amounts given to pupils with additional and special educational needs but without statements. The third is an amount allocated for pupils with statements; this is known as delegated special provision. This section will be divided into three subsections. Initially it will consider the notion of a total special educational needs budget. Secondly, the total AEN/SEN budget for non-statemented pupils will be analysed for each LEA and thirdly how much of the total AEN/SEN budget is delivered by different indices.

Total Special Educational Needs Budget and Delegated Provision for SEN Pupils

A single overall SEN budget heading, which includes cost of special schools and transport of pupils with SEN, has been developed from a proposal by Coopers and Lybrand (1996a). This model has been employed in determining total SEN expenditure from the Section 52 budget statements and includes:

- Total net – Educational Psychology Service/assessments and statementing, as percentage of LSB (1.4.1). (The codes relate to the Section 52 Budget Statement reference).
- Total net – Provision for pupils with statements, as a percentage of LSB (1.4.2)
- Total net – Specialist Support – Pupils with statements, as a percentage of LSB (1.4.3.1)
- Total net – Specialist Support – Pupils without statements, as a percentage of LSB (1.4.3.2)
- Total net – Promoting good practice / collaboration / integration, as a percentage of LSB (1.4.4)
- Total net – Referral Units, as a percentage of LSB (1.4.5.1)
- Total net – Behaviour support plans, as a percentage of LSB (1.4.5.2)
- Total net – Education out of school, as a percentage of LSB (1.4.6)
- Total net – Fees for pupils at independent special schools & abroad, as a percentage of LSB (1.4.8)
- Total net – Inter-authority recoupment, (all schools), as a percentage of LSB (1.10)
- Pupil-led SEN funding – Pupils with statements, as a percentage of LSB
- Pupil-led SEN funding – Pupils without statements, as a percentage of LSB
- Place-led SEN funding, as a percentage of LSB
- Other SEN funding treated as pupil-led, as a percentage of LSB
- Other funding – Additional educational needs factor, as a percentage of LSB

- Pupil-led SEN funding – Pupils with statements, as a percentage of LSB
- Pupil-led SEN funding – Pupils without statements, as a percentage of LSB
- Place-led SEN funding, as a percentage of LSB
- Other SEN funding treated as pupil-led, as a percentage of LSB
- Other funding – Additional educational needs factor, as a percentage of LSB
- Total special ISB, as a percentage of LSB
- Gross – Home to school transport, as a percentage of LSB.

The total SEN spend has increased by 50 per cent, from £2.5 billion in 1996 to £3.8 billion in 2001/02, of which £1 billion is now delegated by English LEAs for AEN/SEN. The range is from 9.9 per cent of the LSB to 23.4 per cent of the LSB and values for each LEA can be obtained from Marsh (2002).

Table 5.3 illustrates the proportions and amounts of the total delegated budget for the four elements of AEN/SEN, i.e. SEN with statements, place led funding treated as pupil led, SEN without statements, and AEN. It should be noted that the CIPFA statistics include pupil and non pupil factors under the AEN heading.

Table 5.3 Delegated AEN/SEN Expenditure for English LEAs 2001/02 (Total £1bn)

	SEN with Statements	Place led funding treated as pupil led	SEN without statements + excess	AEN
Primary	25%	14%	33%	28%
Secondary	31%	11%	31%	27%
Totals	28% £277m	13% £128m	31% £319m	28% £276m

Percentages rounded to nearest integer and therefore may not sum to 100
(source CIPFA Education Statistics)

Table 5.3 shows that 41 per cent of delegated AEN/SEN resources are allocated to pupils with statements in mainstream schools, or to pupils attending special resource units, most of whom have statements (i.e. place led funding treated as pupil led). Further analysis of 2001-02 Section 52 Budget Statements from the CIPFA website indicates that 104 out of 150 LEAs (69 per cent) now delegate either wholly or partially their provision for statements and 89 LEAs (59 per cent) delegate provision for special resource units.

Additional and Special Educational Needs Budget for Pupils with SEN but Without Statements

Within the requirement that 75 per cent of the ISB (changed in 2002/03 from 80 per cent) has to be based on pupil numbers, it is permitted that 5 per cent be allocated on the basis of additional weightings for pupils without statements (Circular 7/91 para. 105). This is sometimes known as the 'hidden 5 per cent' because many LEAs have not made clear in their Section 52 budget statements that this money existed or defined its purpose. Circular 2/94 (DFE, 1994b) states that:

> ...the pupil led component... amounts allocated through additional factors or weightings in respect of non-statemented pupils with SEN may not exceed 5 per cent of the ASB - any further amounts which an LEA proposes to allocate on the basis of additional needs or social deprivation will count against the 20 per cent not allocated on the basis of pupil numbers.

Coopers and Lybrand (1996a) suggested that the 'hidden 5 per cent' should be included in the total SEN calculation. This increases the overall national percentage to 15.3 per cent in line with the amount allocated to AEN by the Standard Spending Assessment. When size of LEA is accounted for, the correlation between total SEN per pupil and the Standard Spending Assessment AEN index score is 0.72. This evidence seems to suggest that there is, at least, some degree of hypothecation in the use of the AEN allowance.

The average amount of funding delegated to schools based on measures of AEN/SEN for pupils without statements is £77 per pupil. The range is from £8 to £270 per pupil. However it would be too simplistic to think that a higher AEN/SEN budget will automatically reduce the budget required for statements without consideration of the issue of accountability. The relationship between AEN/SEN budget allocation and the percentage of statements within each LEA is as low as 0.01 (Marsh,1996).

AEN/SEN Budget Allocations Delivered by the Different Indicators

Analysis of section 52 budget statements shows AEN/SEN budget allocations as being either pupil led under the SEN heading or non-pupil led, under the additional educational needs heading. The resource split is 58 per cent pupil led to 42 per cent non-pupil led. Table 5.4 illustrates the total pupil and non-pupil led amounts for the main AEN/SEN indicators.

Table 5.4   Percentage of LEAs using Indicators for pupils without statements under the Section 52 Budget Statement Headings of SEN and AEN

Indicators	SEN	AEN
Free School Meals	62	75
National Curriculum Assessment	21	12
Tests	21	9
English as an Additional Language	7	20
Pupil Mobility or Turnover	8	15
Number on Roll	13	7
Audit	13	3
Code of Practice	11	5
Baseline Assessment	8	5
Welfare Benefits/Clothing Grants	3	5
Index of Local Deprivation	0	2
Other	6	12

Multiple response table, therefore percentages sum to more than 100

Table 5.4 illustrates the extent to which LEAs have made distinction between pupil led special educational needs and non-pupil led additional educational needs. For example, more LEAs are using National Curriculum Assessments, educational tests, number on roll, Code of Practice stages, and direct pupil audits as indicators within the SEN pupil led component. On the other hand, more LEAs use FSM, English as an additional language and mobility/transience for AEN rather than for SEN.

Table 5.5 Percentage of AEN/SEN Budget Allocated by Different Indicators

Indicators	2002	1997
Free School Meals	47	47
National Curriculum Assessment	8	
Tests	10	11
English as an Additional Language	3	
Pupil Mobility or Turnover	1	
Number on Roll	6	
Audit	13	19
Code of Practice	3	
Baseline Assessment	2	
Welfare Benefits/Clothing Grants	1	
Index of Local Deprivation	0	
Other	5	11
Combined Approaches		12

Percentages rounded up to nearest integer and therefore may not sum to 100

Table 5.5 illustrates the percentage of the AEN/SEN budget allocated by each indicator compared to the 1997 survey (Marsh, 1997a). Table 5.2 has already shown that 96 per cent of LEAs use free school meals for at least one indicator of AEN/SEN. Table 5.5 demonstrates that 47 per cent of the total AEN/SEN budget has been allocated by FSM in both 1997 and 2002. The indicators of direct pupil audit and educational tests allocate a further 23 per cent of the AEN/SEN budget with the remaining 30 per cent being allocated by a combination of other indicators.

What Options are Available for the Distribution of the Extra Resources?

A number of alternative allocation mechanisms have been considered by LEAs to distribute the resources allocated for additional educational needs. These options may be summarised as:

- A flat rate allocation per pupil. This may be regarded as the simplest method, regardless of the type of index chosen, however no account is taken of the different levels of need of individuals/schools.

- A proportional allocation involving the use of thresholds setting a minimum lower and/or upper limit to the percentage of pupils qualifying under the index. A drawback of this type of arrangement is that allocations may be skewed towards certain schools and that SEN pupils in non-qualifying schools will receive nothing.
- Banding, whereby qualifying pupils are identified in a number of bands, which carry different levels of resources. This approach although common, can give rise to the situation in which small differences between pupils/schools can give rise to large differences in funding. However this may be overcome by mathematical devices to smooth allocations.
- Targeting by phase, with a higher weighting given to qualifying pupils/schools in either the primary/secondary phase in order to provide early intervention/enable a wider range of pupil attainments to be addressed across the curriculum.
- Additional amounts for concentrations of AEN e.g. one LEA increased the percentage of FSM to the power of 1.25.

The choice of indicators and the method of resource allocation is clearly an important issue for LEAs and is related to the principle of stability of funding already mentioned in Chapter Three.

Conclusions from the AEN/SEN National Survey

This survey has emphasised the importance of clearly specifying the purpose of additional funding as previously discussed in Chapter Two. It has been shown that more LEAs are using needs related indicators e.g. national curriculum assessments and professional audits/Code of Practice assessment stages than in 1992 and 1997. Also there has been an increase in the number of formula indicators used by LEAs which may imply a higher level of sophistication to the formula. This evidence suggests that LEAs are now beginning to make a distinction in their LMS schemes between funding for special educational needs and funding for social disadvantage.

There has been a general consensus that the proxy socio-economic indicator of free school meals is remarkably robust as a means of predicting incidence levels of pupils with special educational needs and for distributing resources at a school level. It could, indeed, be argued that the principle of simplicity makes this indicator the best option, if accountability for AEN were left out of consideration. The number of LEAs using FSM has increased from 81 per cent to 96 per cent since the first generation of AEN/SEN formulae was surveyed by Lee (1992a). There is still not, however, as much enthusiasm about the continued use of FSM, particularly in the light of the revised Code of Practice which places further emphasis on the identification of special educational needs of individual pupils. The correlation between FSM and SEN at a pupil level falls to 0.20 (Marsh, 1995). For these reasons many LEAs are continuing to review their formulae in an attempt to improve their schemes to a more needs led approach.

As we have seen, free school meals is one of the best SEN indicators for meeting the principles of simplicity and low administrative cost, but performs poorly in terms of responding to individual need. Professional audits and the results of educational tests are better indicators than FSM on a range of principles, particularly if the purpose of additional funding is to focus upon the individual pupil. Audits satisfy the equity principle by attempting to apply consistent standards across schools. They also satisfy the criterion of effectiveness by increasing awareness of good practice targeted at identified pupils. Educational tests are more simple to apply than audits and have lower administrative and maintenance costs. The disadvantage of using tests is the danger of categorising pupils according to particular test cut-off scores, placing an undue emphasis on 'within-child' factors rather than a full consideration of context. The main difference between audits and tests is in the area of cost containment. Audit approaches can be subject to 'identification inflation' which are more difficult to moderate than simple manipulation of test cut-off scores, assuming the school can't influence the test score by the way it administers the test. Chapter Six will examine the different funding arrangements of two LEAs.

LEAs will continue to scrutinise data sources in their future development work in particular, pupil outcomes and indicators of inclusion.

Chapter 6

The Continuum of Funding and Special Educational Needs

The main aim of this Chapter is to examine the relationship between special educational needs (SEN) and resource levels and to consider whether it is worthwhile for LEAs to differentiate financially between different levels of need (Key Questions 6 and 7). The EMIE survey on additional educational needs (Marsh, 2002) reported in Chapter Five, shows that many LEAs distribute their non-statemented SEN resources as a standard unit cost. That is to say, each identified non-statemented SEN pupil is allocated the same amount of money irrespective of the degree and the nature of the learning difficulty. Initially there will be a discussion of the relationship between the continuum of special educational needs and level of provision thought to be required to meet these needs. The second part of the Chapter will consider different approaches to the allocation of non-statemented SEN resources taken by two LEAs. It will draw on qualitative data, including pupil case studies, derived from semi-structured interviews in eight schools which were conducted with headteachers, special educational needs co-ordinators (SENCOs) and heads of department in English, Mathematics and Science. In addition to the main aim other key issues to be addressed will be: the mechanisms for distributing resources for non-statemented special educational needs, the level of and accountability for funding and the use of teaching assistants or outreach teachers.

The Relationship Between the Continuum of SEN and Differentiated Resource Levels

This section will examine in detail the vertical equity principle of providing differentiated funding by looking at the criteria, policies and approaches adopted by the two LEAs (see Marsh, 2000).

Chapter Two has already considered the Code of Practice on the Identification and Assessment of Special Educational Needs (DfES, 2001c) which recognises that there is a continuum of needs, emphasised by the Warnock report (DES, 1978), and a continuum of provision (para. 1:2). The Code of Practice suggests a graduated response to meeting pupils needs within their mainstream school through School Action, School Action Plus, a statutory assessment under section 323 of the 1996 Education Act and where necessary the maintenance of a statement of special educational needs. Although Booth (1994) has questioned the uncritical acceptance of the continua of 'needs' and 'provision', he appeared to be concentrating on the principle of inclusion for all pupils within mainstream education regardless of the severity of their need. The purpose of this Chapter is to provide an investigation into the practice of allocating differentiated levels of resources for pupils with SEN in mainstream schools within the context of providing inclusive education.

If the view of the Warnock committee is accepted that a continuum of SEN exists, then it might be expected that this should be reflected in a continuum of resourcing. Generally, this has not been the case. It has been argued that typically resources are allocated in a discontinuous way to a continuum of needs. One of the outcomes of the 1981 Education Act has been that, whilst the needs of the minority (the 2 per cent or so with statements) have, quite properly, been the focus of much attention, there has not been the same thoroughness in application when dealing with the remaining 18 per cent in mainstream schools.

Policies Towards Differentiated Funding

The relationship between needs and resources is illustrated in Circular 4/73 (DES, 1973) and Circular 11/90 (DES, 1990) and has been examined in Chapter Four. Circular 4/73 was concerned with the more flexible principle of staff-pupil ratios for each category of 'handicap' rather than the rigid concept of class sizes. Circular 11/90, on the other hand, suggested a staffing model which incorporated estimates of staff time, (both teacher and learning support assistants), needed per pupil for five bands of learning difficulty. However this circular made no mention of pupils with special educational needs but without statements.

Some LEAs (e.g. Kent, Northamptonshire and the unitary authorities which were formerly Avon) have attempted to produce integrated special provision arrangements involving professional audits across the full range of special educational needs to include pupils with and without statements (e.g. see Stewart, 1992 and Villette, 1993). The purpose of the audits is to help distribute available funds equitably across schools according to need.

Actual pupils are identified and placed within the continuum of SEN at one of several possible levels. The audit form, therefore, represents a bid for resources and attempts to provide the basis for a consistent and coherent approach to identifying, recording and reviewing pupils' SEN across the LEA. The Department for Education and Skills (DfES) have approved the audit approach if certain criteria are met:

- moderation across the LEA so there are common standards
- evidence to support decisions – simply completing a form is insufficient
- ability to respond to changes – carrying forward the result of an audit from one year to the next unlikely to be acceptable
- the opportunity for some sort of appeal from schools dissatisfied with the outcome of the audit
- random checking of judgements built into the moderation process.

The audit approach has some obvious drawbacks: the time it takes especially at the beginning, the difficulty of making such a process sufficiently objective and consistent and the possibility of perverse incentives so that schools over identify numbers of pupils with SEN to accrue additional resources. Most LEAs have adopted simpler methods. The EMIE survey reported in Chapter Five has indicated that 96 per cent of LEAs use free school meals as a proxy measure of special educational needs. However the survey supports a similar finding by Robertson (1995) that there has been a general movement towards the use of more direct educational criteria for allocating non-statemented SEN resources, either by the use of educational measures such as reading test surveys, national curriculum assessment results or by the use of moderated SEN registers or audits.

Approaches to Differentiated Funding in Two LEAs

The remaining part of this Chapter describes a small scale research study which will examine in detail different approaches taken by two LEAs (*Mercia* and *Whiteshire*) to allocate resources for non-statemented SEN. *Mercia* uses a professional audit and *Whiteshire* makes use of educational measures. The research study had two main objectives:

1. to explore the views of professionals about the different resourcing policies adopted within the two LEAs;

2. to investigate the match between special educational needs and the level of provision thought by professionals to be required to meet these needs.

The wider aim of the study was to examine whether it is worthwhile for LEAs to construct a LMS funding formula for special educational needs to attempt to differentiate financially between different levels of need.

LEA 1 (*Mercia*) is a shire county with a school population of 80,000. It has an average level of pupils (2002 49 per cent) with 5 or more GCSEs at grades A-C and a free school meals entitlement percentage below the national average (11 per cent). LEA 2 (*Whiteshire*) is also a shire county with a school population of 200,000. It also has a percentage of pupils at the national average (2002 51 per cent) with 5 or more GCSEs at grades A-C. *Whiteshire* also has a free school meals entitlement percentage at around the national average (17 per cent).

Four schools were selected within each LEA (8 schools in total) and these were all visited. The intention was not that the sample should be randomly selected but that the schools should be broadly representative of mainstream secondary schools. The four schools from each LEA were divided into two secondaries and two primary/middle. Table 6.1 illustrates the size and school type together with other information relevant to the resourcing of special educational needs pupils.

Table 6.1   AEN/SEN Budgets and FSM Entitlement for schools in the two sample LEAs

School	No on Roll	AEN/SEN Budget £	FSME %	Statement Nos	Statements %
A Secondary	939 Y7-Y11	15,000	10	15	1.6
B Secondary	990 Y7-Y13	9,200	4	12	1.2
C Middle	415 Y5-Y8	8,300	20	17	4.1
D Lower	445 R-Y4	7,100	3	2	0.5
E Secondary	1149 Y7-Y11	154,000	23	45	3.9
F Secondary	851 Y7-Y13	39,900	2	2	0.2
G Junior	279 Y3-Y6	44,600	53	10	3.6
H Primary	239 R-Y6	10,000	11	7	2.9

The next section will provide a descriptive comparison of the level of resources in the two LEAs.

Descriptive Comparison of the Level of Resources within the two LEAs

One of the main differences between the two LEAs is the level of funding which is available for non-statemented special educational needs. Analysis of the Section 52 budget statements which were submitted to the Department for Education and Skills for 2002-03 indicated that *Mercia's* budget for non-statemented SEN pupils is only £50 per pupil compared to *Whiteshire's* £140 per pupil (see Table 6.2). — *good*

Table 6.2   Differences in Funding Amounts in the Two LEAs

LEA	No of Pupils	AEN/SEN Budget per pupil
Mercia	80,000	£50
Whiteshire	200,000	£140

Education officers from *Mercia* claim that 5 per cent of the ISB has already been included in the amount delegated to schools as part of generally available provision. Therefore the AEN/SEN amount per pupil is an artificially low figure. *Whiteshire* does not make this claim.

The effect of these funding arrangements are shown in Table 6.1 which illustrates the non-statemented AEN/SEN budget for the eight schools in the survey. When the secondary schools from the two LEAs are paired together for school type i.e. A and E (Y7-Y11) and, B and F (Y7-Y13), they highlight the large differences in the non-statemented SEN funding. School E receives ten times more in terms of financial support than school A. Similarly, although on a smaller scale, school F receives over four times as much as school B. The differences are not so marked in the primary sector even though direct comparisons are not possible as the four primary/middle schools in the sample are all of different school types and pupil populations and have different free school meal entitlements.

The level of resources in the two LEAs are illustrated further in Table 6.3 which shows the percentage of the pupil population with statements. Despite the relatively high resourcing levels for non-statemented special educational needs in *Whiteshire*, the overall total percentage of statements (4.6 per cent) is considerably more than the 'one child in fifty' as suggested in the 1994 version of the Code of Practice. The comparable statistic for

Mercia is 3.1 per cent of which approximately 40 per cent attend special schools which is a broadly similar percentage to that seen in *Whiteshire* (35per cent).

Table 6.3   Percentage of pupils with statements in special and mainstream schools in Mercia and Whiteshire

	Mainstream Schools	Special Schools	Total
Mercia	1.9 %	1.2 %	3.1 %
Whiteshire	3.0 %	1.6 %	4.6 %

The data in Tables 6.3 and 6.4 suggests that the impact of the higher resourcing levels in *Whiteshire* has not been effective in maintaining and stabilising the statementing rate which are an important element of the total SEN budget. The *SEN Initiative* (Coopers and Lybrand, 1996a) and the Audit Commission (2002) both comment on the increased national pressure for statements of special educational needs, which has also been reflected in *Whiteshire*. The number of statements in the *Whiteshire* increased by an average of 9 per cent per year over the period 1988 to 1998 (see Table 6.4). The increase is explained by the difference between the inflow percentage (i.e. number of new statements) and the outflow percentage (i.e. number of statements which were ceased).

Table 6.4   The Number of Statements in Whiteshire from 1988 to 1998 (source SEN2 returns)

Year	No of Stmts	Yr on Yr Variation	% Yr on Yr Variation	No Stmts issued (inflow)	No Stmts ceased (outflow)
1988	4104			810	
1989	4433	329	8.0%	968	639
1990	4997	564	12.7%	1269	705
1991	5406	409	8.2%	1124	715
1992	5950	544	10.0%	1305	761
1993	6556	606	10.2%	1440	834
1994	7518	962	14.7%	1468	506
1995	8110	592	7.9%	1816	1224
1996	9227	1117	13.8%	2253	1136
1997	9573	346	3.8%	1704	1358
1998	10044	471	4.9%	n/a	n/a

Case Studies to Explore Professional Views about LEA Resourcing Policies for Special Educational Needs

Data Collection Instruments and Interview Procedures

Policy documents were obtained from the two LEAs relating to special educational needs and used as background material about the LEA. Other data was collected by means of a semi-structured questionnaire which the respondents saw prior to the interview and by means of a semi-focused interview. The interviews with the SENCO and heads of departments focused on individual pupils with special educational needs.

Within each secondary school the Headteacher, special educational needs co-ordinator (SENCO), and heads of English, Mathematics and Science were interviewed. Within each primary/middle school the Headteacher and SENCO were interviewed. In one school the Headteacher also took on the role of SENCO.

The professional interviews were transcribed and analysed. Three central themes emerged from the interviews:

policies for funding pupils with special educational needs but without statements;
• designated special provision; and
• learning support assistants or outreach teachers.

Whiteshire had clearly defined outreach teams for the special needs 'categories' of moderate learning difficulties (MLD), specific learning difficulties (SpLD), and emotional and/or behavioural difficulties (EBD). These 'labels' were used in the analysis of the individual pupil data for both authorities.

Policies for Funding Non-Statemented Special Educational Needs : Audit and Formula

Mercia considers that it is important to agree a practical and working definition of terms such as 'special needs' and 'learning difficulty'. The contention is made that only then will it be possible for all schools to define these terms in a consistent way and for the LEA to determine the level and range of needs in each school and to establish a method of funding provision which is widely understood and seen to be fair. *Mercia* has a set of principles within which their SEN policy has been interpreted and developed. Some of the key principles include that:

- provision should be determined by reference to the best interests of the individual pupil though the initial focus of provision should be the mainstream school;
- the segregation or removal of an individual pupil from the local community may diminish the quality of experience for the whole community;
- provision should therefore be aimed to maximise the entitlement of all pupils to the full range of normal experiences in their local community, insofar as this is consistent with the provision of effective education and the efficient use of resources.

The LEA's approach has been to develop a model which is a focus on the *arrangements* made by schools to meet the identified educational needs of pupils, rather than on aspects of need or other within-child factors. It claims explicitly to relate the identification and assessment of special needs to the recording of arrangements made to meet those needs and to the resources required for those arrangements. The arrangements are described in Bands into which children can be placed according to an ascending scale of learning difficulties. At one end of the scale of difficulties (Band 1) are those children with marginal problems – for example, slight reading problems which might be remedied by a small amount of help each day. This would correspond with School Action of the Code of Practice. Band 2 arrangements are those that would correspond to School Action Plus of the Code of Practice Bands 3, 4, 5 and 6 describe increasingly complex special educational arrangements made for pupils with statements of special educational need.

The framework thus attempts to avoid the problems of categorisation of children according to the nature of their needs. The criticism which may be levied at this approach is that the system is really only another labelling device. The question which needs to be asked is whether there are any negative implications for the child, arising from the adoption of the banding arrangements. For instance, how do class/subject teachers perceive a Band 2 pupil as being different from a Band 1 pupil? Do Band 2 pupils only receive segregated 1:1 withdrawal support which may single them out from their peers? The LEA's description of the difference is that the Band 2 pupil should be in receipt of the equivalent of 1 hour of individual teaching support per week. There is no stipulation from the LEA whether the support should be in the form of withdrawal 1:1 provision or in-class support. In practice schools often convert this into 3 hours of Teaching Assistant resources (TA) and the support is given in a combination of methods i.e. 1:1 withdrawal, in-class support and close consultation with the class/subject teacher. When a school wishes to put forward a pupil for proposed Band 2 arrangements, this must be carried out at the time of the annual Audit of Special Educational Needs which takes place during October. A minimum level of evidence is required by the LEA which includes:

- a record of baseline assessment having been carried out and leading to a definition of the priority areas of concern;
- working records giving daily/weekly dated evidence of implementation of the planned programme. These records should be available for at least the second half of the summer term and autumn term (unless the pupil is new to the school);
- programme planning and evaluation sheets to cover the duration of the Band 1 arrangements. The expectation is that these should document programmes for at least the previous term, although again exceptions to this are made for pupils newly arrived to the school.

If it is proposed to move a child from Band 1 to Band 2 then an LEA support teacher would discuss the Band 1 arrangements with the Special Educational Needs Co-ordinator (SENCO). If an agreement is reached the pupil's name is then added to the Band 2 summary sheet under the 'proposed' column. A selection of common measures of attainment are also entered on the summary sheet according to the curriculum area for which the special arrangements have been made. A sample of records for proposed Band 2 pupils are then taken to Agreement Trials which is a panel consisting of Head Teacher, SENCO and support teacher representatives. Their function is to ensure that :

- the guidelines for moving pupils from Band 1 to Band 2 are in place;
- there is consistency in applying the measures within the area teams.

A set of criteria for areas of difficulty is then applied to all the proposed Band 2 pupils. Educational test scores, previously submitted from schools, are used at a second stage of moderation by *Mercia* to provide further evidence for the selection process of which pupils are to be defined as a Band 2 or Code of Practice stage 3. For example, pupils could qualify under any one of 13 'categories' of need. The categories included low scores on the early years checklist, a reading age lower than the tenth percentile, any score on a behaviour checklist or physical difficulties checklist, low attainment target levels in Maths or generally low attainment target levels in the three core subjects of English, Maths and Science. *Mercia* maintained that the high number of 'categories' was necessary to ensure that a wide range of learning difficulties was included.

There appeared to be several encouraging comments about *Mercia*'s overall policies towards special educational needs.

> I think they've got a great desire and willingness to support schools and think its limited purely by the funding they receive. They try very hard to ... they listen to us ... they try very hard to respond to the comments of schools. (Mercia Headteacher)

Other Headteachers from *Mercia* spoke mainly in positive terms about the audit. However there appeared to be a general view that the audit was very time intensive upon teacher time.

> I think what they've tried to do is to focus the need on a basis not measured by free school meals but measured by educational need. I think that would be an area I would welcome ... I think the move of the audit to do that has been helpful not only as much as it's helped to target money in the appropriate direction but it's also helped the school I think, in a way to clarify its own views as to what individual students actually need. So the whole process of completing the audit isn't simply a paper exercise although some schools to be fair have become overwhelmed by the paper work. (Mercia Headteacher)

The comments about the time taken to conduct the audit are repeated by two further respondents.

> ... I was horrified by the amount of paper work that it generated and the amount of time it removed people from the classrooms. That's the biggest concern ... whilst the special needs co-ordinator and her colleagues are working on the audit then quite clearly they are not doing what they should be doing. However the second time round it seemed crisper and didn't seem to take the amount of time I imagined it took in September '93... of course it does mean that we have more funding coming into the school because of the thoroughness of the audit here. So it has been particularly successful in generating special needs ring fenced money. (Mercia Headteacher).

> We're just awash with information, some of which isn't needed and we're spending more time on gathering information than actually doing ... that's the danger. (Mercia SENCO)

Another Headteacher reinforced the view that the time required for the audit could really not be justified in terms of the teacher time taken away from the children.

The audit is a cumbersome process and I've this constant fear that in order to meet audit requirements we are robbing resources that should be going directly to children. This is especially true at Band 2 and I wonder whether we would do better not to comply with the authority arrangements and simply choose to put money in directly to the children and not get the £8000. I often wonder what proportion of the £8000 we spend on administering the authority's arrangements. I have directly asked the group that looks at special needs: have you analysed whether or not the process that you're putting forward actually helps the situation for the children? (Mercia Headteacher)

This fear was supported by another respondent.

I know some schools have kind of voted with their feet and have said we're not going to bother with Band 1 because the money we get is actually not significant compared with the amount of work we have to do in order to get that ... then you get this feeling that it is not about the kids its actually about a lot of other things. (Mercia SENCO).

Other general comments about the audit were: that it was a system in which funding was given retrospectively and the notion was questioned that money should only be given where provision has been documented.

... because it is a retrospective funding system where you spend and get it back later effectively does make you nervous about it and I think that can effect the quality of provision which is given to a child. (Mercia Headteacher)

We as a school have gained significantly in terms of funding from the audit as opposed to through free school meals because part of that is that it is audit of provision and it's catch 22 because you have to be making the provision before you get the funding. We have gained considerably whereas other schools have lost out for example some of the town schools where they a high proportion of children on free school meals have lost money. Now how good that provision was I can't answer but because we make good provision and because we do the audit thoroughly we gain and I'm not altogether sure about that. I'm delighted for our school but it's a lot of work we have to produce mountains of paper work. When the audit was designed I think it was for primary and they don't realise how much pulling together there has to be at a secondary. (Mercia SENCO)

Mercia's revised policy on special educational needs came into effect in 1994. It has received a high profile nationally and has been mentioned in publications referring to good practice. The policy has attempted to make the conceptual shift to move away from a focus on 'within-child' factors, towards an emphasis on the practical arrangements required to meet individual needs. However the policy has not succeeded when viewed in terms of the principle of cost containment. The number of statements in *Mercia* has increased from 2,600 to 3,400 during the period 1996 to 2001.

Whiteshire's SEN statement of policy and practice includes three broad categories of principles:

- general principles for good practice;
- principles for assessment; and
- principles for provision.

Some of the LEA's principles are listed below:

Every pupil should be valued equally and should have access to educational opportunities and a broad and balanced curriculum. For all pupils, the purpose of education is the same, the goals are the same, but the individual children's needs in progressing towards them, will be different.

The LEA will, as a matter of principle, seek to support children with special educational needs in their local mainstream schools.

Resourcing arrangements for SEN should be flexible, recognise the role and responsibilities assigned to schools and support service, and be responsive to the wishes of parents.

Each school should demonstrate a commitment to meeting the SEN of its whole school population, and should develop a whole school approach to pupils with SEN which reflects the school's commitment to the curriculum entitlement of all pupils.

Pupil access to educational resources should be determined by individual needs. Provision should be flexible and responsive to the assessed and changing needs of children.

Whiteshire use educational tests with 'cut-off' criteria rather than administering a professional audit to distribute the allocation for non-statemented special educational needs. There is a separate formula for the primary and secondary sectors known as the primary and secondary SEN index. In general terms the primary index uses a balance of educational and social disadvantage factors whereas the secondary index only incorporates educational tests. Following an extensive review of the secondary index it was recommended that a social disadvantage factor should be included to bring it into line with the primary formula, including the possible use of National Curriculum Assessment results (NCA). The proposed revised formula included group eligibility to educational welfare benefits (EWB) weighted at 25 per cent. The remaining 75 per cent would be allocated on the basis of educational special needs factors which would incorporate NCA.

The second important theme to be identified from the professional interviews was the policy of delegated special provision which applied to *Mercia.*

Delegated Special Provision : Allocation of Resources for Statements

As already discussed in the previous section the proportion and number of pupils with statements has steadily increased since the implementation of the 1988 Education Act (see Table 6.4 and also Marsh, 1997b, 1999). The proportion of pupils with statements who attend mainstream schools has also increased significantly. Norwich (1994) reported that in 1992 over 40 per cent of pupils with statements aged 5-15 years were in mainstream schools in England with a considerable variation across the LEAs, from 11 per cent in East Sussex to 84 per cent in Cornwall. In an updated report Norwich (2002) reported that in 2001 64 per cent of pupils with statements aged 5 to 15 years were in mainstream schools. Also in 2001 76 per cent of pupils with statements made for the first time were placed in a mainstream school (Table 11 DfES, 2002c). Despite the increase in mainstream statements it is significant to note that the number of pupils educated in special schools in England remained virtually constant during the period 1991 to 1997 (DfEE, 1997b). More recent statistics illustrate there has been a slight reduction in the percentage of pupils placed in special schools from 1.2 per cent in 1997 to 1.1 per cent in 2002 (Table 14 DfES, 2002c). In *Whiteshire* there has been a slight reduction in the percentage of pupils attending special schools during the period 1997 to 2002 (1.3 per cent to 1.2 per cent) whereas in *Mercia,* during the same time period, there has been a slight increase from 0.9 per cent to 1.0 per cent.

Initially mainstream schools in *Whiteshire* received additional support to provide for pupils with statements largely through the development of outreach support teams. Sometimes the outreach teams were attached to particular special schools, existing support service teams or units. A major weakness of the arrangements is that since the outreach staff are deployed from individual schools, units or services rather than on a District or Area basis, a mainstream school might have had statemented pupils supported by different outreach teachers from different locations. Additionally the mainstream school was not involved in selection or recruitment of outreach staff. This led to difficulties for the mainstream schools in their management of a coherent whole school policy and practice for SEN. As schools' confidence has grown in the area of supporting pupils with statements, particularly within secondary schools, *Mercia* and *Whiteshire* now delegate resources to enable schools to build on their current progress and promote the inclusion of pupils with SEN. The EMIE survey (Marsh, 2002) indicated that at 2001/02 104 out of 150 LEAs (69 per cent) delegate either wholly or partially their provision for statements. The policy of delegation for statements can require the authority to determine the number of places it is to fund for pupils with statements each year or the LEA can allocate a unit value for each pupil with a statement. Although this delegation is aimed at pupils with statements, pupils with special educational needs but without statements may also benefit if they are in the same class or subject grouping as the pupils receiving the additional support.

Mercia Headteachers generally spoke very favourably about the delegation arrangements and felt that the initiative had enhanced the life of the school. It made planning much more effective and enabled the school to build up expertise in particular areas.

> I think that the designated special provision arrangement is a good initiative. It's an arrangement that we know very clearly where we stand. Taking on the delegation arrangements has enhanced our own special needs provision. It's given it a solid base which I don't think we would have achieved without it. It has also enhanced the life of the school as well because in taking it on we have attracted a number of other children to the school. We have a child with cerebral palsy, we have couple of Asperger Syndrome children all of whom have added to the life of the school. We want to extend with another specification possibly on the autism continuum and we want to develop expertise there. (Mercia Headteacher)

The field work was conducted when delegation in *Whiteshire* was at the consultation stage with schools, teacher association and governing bodies. The two secondary headteachers from *Whiteshire* were supportive of the proposal but concerns were mentioned about the efficiency of resources, in particular about the use of non teaching assistants instead of outreach teachers. This theme will be considered in more detail in the next section.

> I'm generally in favour but however my only concern is that if it is delegated to secondary schools to what extent they will employ the outreach teachers who are working in those schools at the minute. They may well go down the road of non-teaching assistants because it's so much cheaper and whether that will produce as good an outcome is anybody's guess. We certainly value the

outreach teachers we have but whether the school will be able to employ four of them is another matter. (Whiteshire Headteacher).

Teaching Assistants or Outreach Teachers

A major difference between the two LEAs is the use and employment of classroom assistants or Teaching Assistants to support both pupils with statements and pupils with special educational needs but without statements. Under the delegation arrangements *Mercia* schools have the flexibility to purchase teaching assistants (TAs) or outreach teachers. The case study schools have converted the four hours of teaching time to twelve hours of non-teaching or TA time. In *Whiteshire*, for historical reasons, a much greater reliance is made upon outreach teachers. Having employed qualified teachers since the implementation of the 1981 Education Act in 1983, understandably the teacher associations in *Whiteshire* are sceptical and resistant to any change in the current arrangements.

The employment of teaching assistants has increased rapidly since the implementation of the 1981 Education Act and is still growing (Goacher et al, 1988). The decision by the two LEAs whether to employ teaching assistants appeared to be based on the level of funding which was seen to be available to schools. As Lorenz (1992) points out:

> Thus whether resources for children with special needs have been delegated to schools by the LEA or retained centrally, the need to make 'efficiencies' has become a predominant consideration. Clearly by employing assistants rather than teachers or even nursery nurses, schools and LEAs can make real savings.

Respondents from *Mercia* took the view cited by Lorenz, that it was more cost effective to employ teaching assistants in terms of the numbers of personnel which could be employed. This could be interpreted as implying that the 'hidden 5 per cent' in *Mercia*'s budget did not seem to have an impact on the level of spending by schools. The effectiveness of using non-teaching staff was also often questioned.

> We've got a number of classroom assistants who are well meaning people who come on a APT&C scale. We've done some training with them that has been organised by the LEA for the local schools. They are very useful and very helpful but obviously they haven't got quite the education experience that teachers have got ... It would be much more costly but perhaps a lot more effective to have an additional teacher in the classroom but of course that is something we can't afford to do to any great extent. (Mercia Headteacher)

We have a very good team of special needs assistants some of whom literally walked in off the streets but have been trained up in house and I think deliver a very successful support team network ... I don't think that special needs has been funded sufficiently well and one example I suppose would be the reason the school has continued to employ unqualified people instead of special needs qualified teachers because you can employ half a dozen classroom assistants against one teacher. I would argue we need both for very different purposes. (Mercia Headteacher)

... our Year 8 pupils are in four sets. Next year for financial reasons they've got to be in three and we're looking at a bottom set of 25 kids which may or may not be supported. It's always an annual sort of ... we have to put forward what we'd like in terms of support but it's the quality of that support. And that's no disrespect to the special needs assistants but I think when you've got 25 in there you need special needs teachers as well as yourself to team teach. I think that's really a quite dynamic way of doing it. (Mercia Head of Mathematics)

Similar concerns have been expressed by Baskind and Thompson (1995) who stated that if schools and LEAs are beginning to employ cheaper, non-professional personnel to support the teaching and learning systems set up in individual institutions, they should be aware that to date there is little research into the effectiveness of this group of educationalists.

Other important issues which are pertinent to the use of either type of support in the classroom are the 'ownership' of special educational needs pupils and a perceived inefficient use of resources whereby there may be more than one support member of staff in the classroom.

My concern about that is that it deskills the mainstream teacher because he or she is likely to say those students are your concern ... How do you make 50 odd colleagues aware of the Code of Practice without beating them metaphorically with it, because of course that means people don't read they look at documents or whatever. But how do we increase the awareness and avoid at the same time the deskilling that I referred to earlier – because I do see that as a serious issue in some of my colleagues ... the special needs children are not my concern I've got a classroom assistant here ... she (sic) will deal with it. (Mercia Headteacher)

HMI's reported back from one school in *Whiteshire* that on more than one occasion they noted the presence of three teachers in a class: the class teacher, support teacher and an outreach teacher.

The one criticism they made (HMI visit) is very difficult to put right if we stick with the same system. That is they thought there was a certain amount of duplication of effort between our support teachers and the outreach teachers who were ostensibly there to work with statemented pupils. But because we know the outreach teachers very well ... we have four outreach teachers who work full time here and are not dotting about, they regard themselves as members of our staff and I've encouraged them to do that and because of that they don't limit themselves to the one or two statemented pupils, so in some classrooms there may be three teachers. (Whiteshire Headteacher)

The question of whether teaching assistants (TAs) or outreach teachers should be employed is clearly a sensitive issue. Although the use of TAs could be justified on efficiency grounds, the main criterion for evaluation should be effectiveness. It was clear that respondents from *Mercia* had doubts in this area. As a post script to the study *Whiteshire* has since adopted a three level system to grade and remunerate the skills and experience of the teaching assistant. This is an attempt to provide a better focus for the resources.

Mercia and *Whiteshire's* policies for funding non-statemented special educational needs show important differences in style and approach and are illustrative of the two theoretical perspectives used in this book. Although both LEA's policies attempt to identify individual pupils experiencing SEN, *Mercia's* professional audit, maps more readily onto the 'school and teacher effectiveness' discourse by focussing on the teaching arrangements. *Whiteshire's* use of educational tests is more typical of the 'special needs pupil' discourse as the emphasis is upon deficits within the child i.e. low performance in tests.

Mercia also recognised a window of opportunity and created a climate for change not only in resourcing special educational arrangements but also in the management structure of SEN. On the other hand *Whiteshire* took a more considered stance and preferred to hold onto the historical approach to funding, arguing that the most important feature of the SEN formula was stability of funding. This viewpoint was taken to encourage schools to remain within the LEA rather than to seek grant maintained status under the terms of the 1988 Education Act.

Individual Pupil Case Studies to Explore Professional Views about the Match between Special Educational Needs and Resource Levels

This section will now consider individual pupil case studies, firstly to provide further exemplification and comparison of the two LEAs' policies; secondly, to furnish evidence on the important issue of the extent to which professionals can agree the matching of resource levels to need.

Different levels of additional teaching arrangements provided for both statemented and non-statemented SEN pupils were examined within each of the eight schools (two secondary and two primary schools from each LEA). In addition to the LEA records of the number of statements, *Whiteshire* also kept data on which type of learning need support (mainstream and special) was specified on a pupils' statement, see Table 6.5.

Table 6.5   Percentage of overall statements within Whiteshire by type of learning need

Type of Learning Support	Percentage of pupil population with statements
Moderate Learning Difficulties	1.7 %
Specific Learning Difficulties	1.3 %
Emotional and/or Behavioural Difficulties	0.6 %
Severe Learning Difficulties	0.3 %
Physical Difficulties	0.3 %
Visual/Hearing Impairment	0.2 %
Other	0.2 %
Total	4.6 %

Table 6.6 shows the cash values for a pupil with significant learning and/or behavioural difficulties in the two LEAs. *Mercia* attempted to rationalise the funding value by first deciding on the cost of SEN arrangements for pupils with statements. The assumption was made that for each group of 10 pupils the following resources were required (using 2002 salary costs):

- 1 teacher (i.e. approximately £30,000 to include on-costs);
- 1 Nursery Nurse (NNEB) (i.e. approximately £19,000 to include on-costs);
- administrative time;
- fixed equipment.

The total cost for 10 pupils was estimated to be £66,000 or £6,600 for each pupil. *Mercia* then used this weighting (6.6) as the base for funding up to Year 2 pupils i.e. 6.0 multiplied by the age weighted pupil unit (AWPU) £1440. Slightly different weightings were applied to the different age groups: e.g. Y3-Y6 and Y7-Y9 . These weightings therefore included the AWPU and an additional element for special educational needs which took account of the increased AWPU for secondary pupils. Table 6.6 shows that in *Mercia* and *Whiteshire* the resource levels for a primary pupil were similar to those for a secondary pupil. The provision needed for a pupil with a statement was calculated using a base of 0.1 of a teacher. The value of £3,000 (i.e. £30,000*0.1) used in Table 6.6 was explained by one Headteacher:

> The top of the scale is about £26,000 and then there are on-costs of 15¾per cent. There are also other costs built into the formula: he or she attracts a share of adult meals, a share of travelling expenses, a share of recruitment expenses and quite importantly he or she also attracts a share of the incentive allowance scheme which is over and above the average salary. The overall cost of a teacher is therefore about £30,000.

Table 6.6   Resource levels for pupils with statements in Mercia and Whiteshire

Age	Mercia			Whiteshire		
	AWPU	Funding for Smt	Total	AWPU	Funding for Smt	Total
Y6	£1440	£4040	£5480	£1440	£3000	£4440
Y7	£2040	£3350	£5390	£1770	£2750	£4520

To examine the relationship between individual pupils' needs and the resourcing level received a small sample of pupils from each school were selected, (total n=73). This sample included both pupils with statements and pupils with special educational needs but without statements. Information was collected by completion of a proforma during the interviews with the SENCOs and head of departments. The pupils were chosen by the SENCOs to be a descriptive but not necessarily representative sample.

The sample of 73 pupils selected by the SENCOs were of the following learning types:

• MLD n=38

- EBD n=16
- SpLD n= 9
- Other n=10
  (i.e. speech and language difficulty =3; physical difficulties =3; visual impairment = 2; hearing impairment = 1; medical conditions =1).

As noted previously in this Chapter, *Whiteshire* used learning categories to determine the type of outreach teaching support to be delivered to a particular pupil. Illustrative case studies and quantitative data for each of the three main learning difficulty areas as indicated in Table 6.5, i.e. moderate learning difficulties, specific learning difficulties and emotional and/or behavioural difficulties, will be provided to include both pupils with special educational needs but without statements and pupil with statements. The conclusion will provide a discussion as to whether these learning categories are useful in practice for resource allocation or whether they are against the spirit of the 1981 Education Act. Professional views will be explored about the match between special educational needs and actual resource levels, (n.b. a school week is taken as 25 hours unless otherwise stated).

Apart from the greater percentage of pupils with statements in *Whiteshire,* both in the LEA as a whole and in the sample, the other main difference is the percentage of pupils ascertained to be at School Action Plus. The percentage of School Action Plus pupils in *Mercia* is more than double the percentage of these pupils in *Whiteshire.* This seems to suggest that the funding mechanism employed by the two LEAs does play a significant role in shaping a school's response to the Code of Practice and to which stage a pupil might be placed. In *Mercia* schools complete their audit in order to gain access to more resources from the LEA for their School Action Plus (Band B) pupils. In *Whiteshire* the cash resources have already been allocated to the schools by way of the educational test results and there is no further resource advantage in designating them as School Action Plus. One might predict from the higher percentage of School Action Plus pupils in *Mercia* that the LEA would find themselves with an increase in the number of requests for statutory assessment initiations when the two termly reviews at School Action Plus have taken place and the evidence suggests that unsatisfactory progress has been made. This assertion is supported from evidence from DfES statistics signifying an increase in the number of statements from 2,800 to 3,300 during the period 1997 to 2002 (DfES, 2002c).

Moderate Learning Difficulties

Table 6.7 indicates the additional teaching and non-teaching hours which have been allocated to individual pupils (n=38) who are at a variety of different Code of Practice stages. The cost column has been calculated to estimate the equivalent amount in pounds per year of the additional teacher and/or LSA hours. On-costs of approximately 21 per cent have been included to allow for national insurance/superannuation contributions. One teacher hour for one pupil was calculated as being equivalent to approximately £30 i.e. £30,000 / (25 hours * 38 weeks). There appeared to be a variety of remuneration costs for LSA in the two LEAs. If the TA had a nursery nurse qualification (NNEB), then the National Joint Council (NJC) scale was used, points 16 to 23, which at 2002 was approximately £13,200 to £16,200. An estimate of one TA hour for one pupil was therefore calculated as being equivalent to approximately £10 i.e. £9,500 / (25 hours * 38 weeks).

The additional assumption was made that if the support was given in-class then at least one other pupil in the class group would also benefit to a similar amount. In reality the additional support may in fact be shared by a several other pupils. The other assumption is that there are 25 hours available in a school week for support and 38 academic weeks per year.

Example of cost calculation per year
Pupil A   0 hours of teacher support per week
            13 hours of TA support per week
Cost = [(No of teacher support hrs*£25/gp size) + (no of LSA hrs*£10/gp size)]*38wks
Cost = [(0*£30/not defined) + (13*£10/2)]*38 = £2470

Table 6.7 Pupils assessed as experiencing moderate learning difficulties

School	Year	CoP	RA	CT hours	Gp size	TA hours	Gp size	Prof asses	Cost £
A	8	5	6.11	5	2	1	2	ok	3040
F	7	5	10.00	2.75	2	0	1	ok	1568
A	7	5	8.06	0	1	17	2	ok	3230
B	7	5	7.09	0	1	12	2	ok	2280
B	7	5	7.06	0	1	12	2	ok	2280
A	7	5	6.11	0	1	16	2	ok	3040
A	7	5	6.10	0	1	17	2	ok	3230
H	4	5	6.07	5	5	0	1	ok	1140
H	4	5	6.05	5	3	0	1	ok	1900
D	4	5	6.03	0	1	10	2	ok	1900
H	2	5	6.06	2	6	0	1	less	380
D	2	5	5.09	0	1	10	2	ok	1900
H	2	5	6.06	1	6	0	1	less	190
A	10	3	10.00	2	2	2	1	ok	1900
A	9	3	9.08	3	2	3	2	ok	2280
A	9	3	8.07	1	5	2	2	ok	608
B	7	3	9.02	0	1	6	2	ok	1140
B	7	3	8.11	0	1	0	2	more	0
B	7	3	7.11	4	1	0	1	more	4560
H	6	3	8.06	2.5	3	0	1	ok	950
H	5	3	8.01	2.5	4	0	1	ok	713
G	5	3	7.06	10	2	5	2	more	6650
H	5	3	7.00	2.5	4	0	1	ok	713
C	5	3	6.06	0	1	2	2	ok	380
H	4	3	7.03	2	4	0	1	ok	570
H	2	3	6.06	2	6	0	1	ok	380
H	1	3	<6.00	4	6	0	1	ok	760
A	10	2	10.06	0	1	2	2	ok	380
A	7	2	10.00	0	1	16	2	ok	3040
A	9	1	10.06	2	2	0	1	ok	1140
A	8	1	10.00	4	2	0	1	ok	2280

Age Weighted Pupil Unit (AWPU) cost has not been included, see Table 6.6
Schools A to D are from Mercia (M) and Schools E to H are from Whiteshire (W)
Professional assessment indicates whether the teacher was satisfied with the level of support (ok), thought the support was too generous (less) or thought that more support was required (more)

The remaining part of this section will present a sub-sample of individual pupil vignettes to illustrate the professional assessment of resource levels with actual levels of support. These individual case studies will concentrate on the costing of resource levels and will provide evidence to answer Key Question 6 i.e. what is the relationship between special educational needs and resource levels and how does this match professional views?

The conclusion will be drawn that there appears to be no professional consensus about the levels of resources required for the different 'types' of need or for the different levels of need. As expected the amount of resource is generally greater for pupils with statements than for pupils at School Action Plus. However significant anomalies exist for the resource levels both thought to be required and currently designated for pupils of similar levels of learning difficulty. The evidence to answer Key Question 6 has been obtained from within the framework of the 'special needs pupil' discourse. However that is not to undermine the importance of the 'school and teacher effectiveness' discourse i.e. by providing suitably differentiated curriculum materials and the evaluation of specialised teaching approaches/strategies.

Joe (Mercia) Y7. Joe has a statement for moderate learning difficulties. The official allocation from *Mercia* is £5,390. This was interpreted by the school as being the equivalent to 4 hours of individual teaching support i.e. £30,000 *4/25 or roughly equivalent to £4,800. A conversion then took place to 12 hours of teaching assistant support or TA. The resource estimate in the 'cost' column has been calculated to be £2280 because the TA is in practice shared by the whole class and the assumption has been made that at least one other pupil receives an equivalent amount of support. This was explained by the SENCO.

> Joe gets 4 hours teacher support which has been determined by the statement. This has been converted to 12 hours of classroom assistant support. This is difficult to organise because of his timetable in that it tends to be an academic subject then a practical subject then an academic. So it's difficult to organise support. Obviously he doesn't need the support in practical subjects usually. I am happy with this level of support especially as I've combined it with another statemented pupil in the same class and so there's an additional adult in the room at all times and really you cannot use one adult with a student for the whole lesson because they lose their independence.

Owen (Whiteshire) Y7. Owen also has a statement for moderate learning difficulties. He has received outreach support from a teacher attached to the moderate learning difficulties special school. During the current academic year this was for a total of 2¾ hours which comprised of 1 hour in a class of 30 for History, 1 hour of individual teaching during Physics, and ¾ of an hour during Information Technology in a class of 16. His current literacy attainment levels at the start of the Summer term were approximately at the ten year level which would correspond to the twentieth percentile. The cost of his provision is assessed at £1,568.

Ruth (Mercia) Y9. Ruth is assessed by the school to be at Code of Practice School Action Plus and is considered to be experiencing mild learning difficulties. She receives 6 hours of in class support per week i.e. 3 hours of teacher support and 3 hours of classroom assistant support (cost £2,280). Her reading attainments were assessed as being at the nine and a half level which would correspond to the tenth percentile. The head of the English Department described the teaching arrangements for his subject:

> Ruth is in a group of 16 students and in Year 8, 9 onwards we put students in sets. She's in set 4 out of 4. Out of the 16 students one is statemented and 10 of the other students are at School Action or School Action Plus. So there are a lot of students in the group who have got different types of learning difficulties and some behavioural difficulties as well but they're lively bright kids and they can be quite a handful. I have three lessons with the group and I have support from a teacher for two of the three. One lesson I don't have any support. We have individual study programmes for the students and the support teacher has designed these. Ideally I would like support in all three lessons.

Although the majority of the professional assessments indicated a satisfaction with the levels of resource there are significant inconsistencies in the continuum of provision for pupils experiencing moderate/mild learning difficulties. For example Ruth, who is assessed to be at School Action Plus, has more provision than Joe who has the protection of a statement. These pupils are from the same LEA but attend different schools.

The evidence from Table 6.7 suggests that the professional opinion about the required level of support for pupils with similar levels of learning difficulty is very varied. For example, *Susan* and *Darren*, who are both in Year 5 and at School Action Plus, have reading attainments of between 7 years 0 months and 7 years 6 months and are allocated very different levels of resource when costed on an annual basis. *Susan* receives 10 hours of in-class teacher support and 5 hours in-class TA support compared to *Darren* who only receives 2½ hours of teacher support in a group of 4 pupils. Despite *Susan*, receiving the cost equivalent of £6,650, and having higher reading attainments, it is considered by the SENCO that more support is required, whereas the professional view of *Darren's* cost equivalent of £713, is felt to be satisfactory. Further inconsistencies in the continuum of provision for pupils experiencing moderate/mild learning difficulties are illustrated by the three pupil vignettes. These pupils are from the same LEA (*Mercia*) but attend different schools. In *Whiteshire, Owen* also has a statement, but his learning difficulties, as measured by reading attainments, are in fact at the twentieth percentile and the cost of the resource (£1,568) is less than *Ruth's* stage 3 resource level (£2,280).

Specific Learning Difficulties

Although information from *Mercia* was not available for the numbers of pupils with statements for specific learning difficulties as obtained for *Whiteshire* in Table 6.5, it soon became clear that there was a large difference between the practice of the two LEAs. For example, of the 12 statements in secondary school B in *Mercia* there were no pupils experiencing specific learning difficulties, eleven were for pupils experiencing moderate learning difficulties and there was one visually impaired pupil. Secondary school E in *Whiteshire* received specific learning difficulty outreach teaching support for 28 pupils out of the 45 statements. Table 6.3 indicates that there were 3.0 per cent of pupils with statements receiving their support in the mainstream school in *Whiteshire* compared to 1.9 per cent in *Mercia*. The 1.1 per cent difference seems to be made up of mainly specific learning difficulty pupils as indicated in Table 6.5.

Table 6.8 Pupils assessed as experiencing specific learning difficulties

School	Year	CoP Stage	RA	CT hours	Group size	TA hours	Group size	Prof assess	Cost £
A	11	5	8.07	4	1	0	1	ok	4560
E	9	5	10.10	5	2	0	1	less	2850
E	9	5	10.10	5	2	0	1	ok	2850
F	8	5	9.04	1	1	0	1	less	1140
A	8	5	7.01	5	2	5	2	ok	3800
G	5	5	7.06	2	1	10	2	more	4180
C	5	3	6.08	0	1	2	2	more	380
D	4	3	7.00	2	4	3	4	more	855
G	4	3	6.03	10	2	5	2	more	6650

Note : Age Weighted Pupil Unit (AWPU) cost has not been included.

Peter (Whiteshire) Y8. Peter receives individual support from a specific learning difficulties outreach teacher for one hour per week. His reading attainments are approximately at the nine and half year level or approximately at the tenth percentile. His cognitive abilities were assessed as being within the low average range of abilities. His learning difficulties are not considered to be significant by the school. The cost of his provision is assessed at £1,140.

> He gets 1 lesson of outreach teaching support per week ... It seems to me that there any other pupils with a far greater need, whilst we acknowledge that it's been useful for Peter we just find it unusual that he's getting that level of support. He's just weak academically but he's a very willing lad, very nice lad, he'll always do his homework and do it to the best of his ability but he's just weak across the board ... He's not what I would regard one of the difficult pupils at all in terms of learning (SENCO).

Tina (Mercia) Y4. Tina has been assessed to be at School Action Plus. Her reading attainments are at the seven year level or approximately at the tenth percentile. She is fortunate to be in a class where there is a higher level of support than in other classes in the school. The cost of her provision is assessed at £855.

> She gets both teacher and non-teacher support because all the year 4 Band 2's are in the same class so they get a tremendous amount of support.... so that the teacher for certain parts of some days has got an extra teacher and an ancillary.... the teacher can plan her days when that happens. So Tina will have

at least the equivalent of two hours individual help per week. If her group size is 4 then she'll get the equivalent of 8 hours. The size of the groups will vary according to needs. In practice it look like 2.5 hours teacher support and 3 hours ancillary. The group sizes vary from 3 to 5. I think 2 hours per week even if it was individual support is not good enough really... she would need some more because to do her best somebody at least to prompt her and to keep her on task. (Headteacher)

Table 6.8 indicates the significant differences in the levels of support which were available in the sample schools for pupils with a statement and at School Action Plus. There does not appear to be a professional agreement as to an appropriate level of resourcing for pupils who appear to have similar attainment levels. For example, *Tina* and *Peter* both have reading attainments assessed at approximately the tenth percentile. *Tina* is assessed to be at School Action Plus whereas *Peter* has a statement. Another pupil in the same year group as *Tina* is pupil *Andy*. *Andy*, has been assessed to be at School Action Plus, and is shown to have the cost equivalent of £6,650 compared to *Peter* whose cost equivalent is £1,140. *Peter's* time is considered by the school to be excessive whereas pupil *Andy's* school feel that more support is needed than is presently available.

Emotional and/or Behavioural Difficulties

This area of learning difficulties was considered by the majority of respondents to be particularly important as very often there were significant hidden costs involved. These costs were often in addition to any teacher/TA support time which was allocated. One SENCO commented that in one week she had been involved in 12 hours of meetings and telephone discussions with: the pupil, parents, school staff and other professional agencies. None of this time was specified in the pupil's individual education plan as support time.

Mercia recognised EBD within their audit arrangements by requesting schools to complete a behaviour checklist for any pupils considered to be at Band 2 (School Action Plus). Following a moderation exercise any pupil selected for support would receive the Band 2 unit value of £500. *Whiteshire* did not recognise EBD directly in their formula but considered that such pupils would be identified *de facto* by the factors within the formula. However concern was shown by respondents in *Whiteshire* about the unitary resourcing costs.

In terms of teacher time you've got a situation whereby an MLD child can be quite happily catered for in a group but very often an EBD child, because of the nature of the problem, needs the attention of the individual teacher surprisingly often. So I could happily sustain an argument that said an EBD child would attract more money than a MLD child or a SpLD child who can be handled in a group situation. Now when you get your EBD child you can't put that child in a group like that. He/she requires individual support and the time has got to be made available after play-times, after dinner-times when they can come in and let steam off. You're talking counselling in a sense. (Headteacher)

Table 6.9   Pupils   assessed   as   experiencing   emotional   and/or behavioural difficulties

School	Year	CoP	RA	CT hours	Group size	TA hours	Group size	Prof assess	Cost £
B	9	5	10.06	4	2	0	1	more	2280
G	6	5	11.01	1	2	0	1	more	570
A	8	4	8.04	1	1	7	2	more	2470
C	6	4	8.07	0	1	6	2	more	1140
A	11	3	10.00	0	1	3	2	ok	570
A	10	3	8.07	2	2	1	1	more	1520
E	9	3	10.10	0	1	0	1	more	0
B	9	3	10.06	0	1	6	2	ok	1140
B	9	3	10.06	0	1	0	1	more	0
B	9	3	10.03	0	1	6	2	more	1140
F	9	3	10.00	0	1	0	1	more	0
F	9	3	9.00	0	1	0	1	more	0
F	8	3	10.06	0	1	0	1	more	0
F	7	3	10.06	0	1	0	1	more	0
E	7	3	10.01	0	1	0	1	more	0
G	3	3	6.00	0	1	3	6	more	190

Note: Age Weighted Pupil Unit (AWPU) cost has not been included.

The actual teaching arrangements for a pupil (David) considered to be at School Action Plus experiencing emotional and behavioural difficulties were described by a SENCO. The cost of David's provision is assessed at £190.

David (Y3) 'He does not get a lot of direct support. He works in a group of 5 or 6 with a NTA for 3 hours a week for his learning difficulties. The classteacher and I have worked together on some behaviour programmes and the classteacher has instigated a home/school book for behaviour. He needs an experienced EBD teacher for possibly two separate hours per hours week preferably to work on a 1:1 basis at least at the beginning and doing a lot of personal and social education, social skills and making friends and considering other people and that sort of thing. I don't think a NTA could provide the individual support. A NTA could provide support in the class if one of the targets was staying in his seat, or shouting out but I think the actual programme of work would need to be developed by someone more experienced'.

This was the only area of learning difficulties within the case study which provided a consistent level of agreement between the teachers who were consulted. Table 6.9 illustrates that in 14 out of the 16 pupils, identified as experiencing emotional and/or behavioural difficulties, the professional view judged that more support or resources were required to meet the pupils needs. However a certain ambivalence prevailed in that seven of the pupils, all of secondary age, did not receive any additional support at all, despite being selected by the SENCOs as causing a high level of concern within the school for behavioural reasons.

Evaluative Comparison of the Two LEAs

The differences in LEA funding mechanisms have already been discussed in detail in Chapter Five. This Chapter has highlighted and contrasted two approaches, namely the audit and educational tests. I shall now use the principles or criteria listed in Chapter Three to provide an evaluative comparison.

With respect to the criterion of administrative simplicity, *Mercia's* audit is a complicated and complex process which requires a team of trained LEA support teachers to moderate the requests from schools for a higher level of arrangements for particular pupils. The handbook of guidance provided to *Mercia's* schools although comprehensive and time consuming, does meet the principle of procedural equity i.e. there is a consistent application of agreed rules. Vertical equity, however is not met as there is no differentiation of funding. The criterion of effectiveness is dependent on the purpose of allocating additional resources and it is not clear from the LEA's policy documents whether *Mercia* wished to raise educational achievement for SEN pupils or to provide compensatory resourcing for social disadvantage.

The main advantage of the audit approach is that it is founded on a professional assessment of pupil need based on the arrangements which schools should make to meet those needs. In this respect it links in extremely well with the Code of Practice and the principle of responsiveness to needs. The main criticism about the audit has been the time necessary to complete the procedures and therefore it can be said to be inefficient. If the main purpose of the audit is perceived by schools to be a method of distributing resources then support for its bureaucracy is going to be limited, simply because the level of resources is relatively low. However the LEA has played a major role in promoting and marketing the audit as a formative and summative assessment technique which provides a focus on the identification of children's needs. This should be of value to the school when drawing up an individual education plan for a particular pupil. The reality is, of course, despite the statutory duties towards pupils with special educational needs as required from the 1996 Education Act and 2001 SEN and Disability Act, in practice schools do afford different priority levels to SEN. If SEN is placed of high value and given adequate resource levels by the governing body, then it is likely that the audit will have a positive impact within a school. On the other hand if SEN is not given such a high priority then there is more chance that the audit will be viewed as an unnecessary additional administrative exercise.

The principle of stability of funding has been approached by using transition arrangements to change over from the previous system of allocation by free school meals data to the audit. For example in Year 1 25 per cent of the available budget was allocated by the audit and 75 per cent by the free school meals. In Year 2 the proportion was set as 50 per cent: 50 per cent until in Year 4 the whole budget for non-statemented SEN was allocated by the audit. The principle of cost containment in *Mercia* has not been met as the percentage of statements has continued to increase.

In general terms *Mercia's* audit approach does offer the possibility for sharper accountability as schools record the teaching arrangements made for individual pupils. However there was still concern expressed by respondents from *Mercia* about the issue of accountability and about the presentation of the formula.

I think it would help if the 5 per cent was a transparent part of the formula. I was trying to look yesterday ... to see if I could find that clearly identified in any of the financial regulations, building up the formula ... but I couldn't quickly find it ... so it's not I think, publicised enough that this sum of money should actually be allocated for specific special needs. (Mercia Headteacher)

Whiteshire, in comparison, have used an 'off the peg' assessment approach which utilises previous assessment practices adopted by the LEA over the years. The advantage of this approach is that the measures are objective and simple to implement and are not subject to 'observer bias', whereby there has been a tendency for the numbers of pupils identified by the audit to increase year to year because of the link with resource allocation. The disadvantage of using tests is that the use of cut-off scores may present dangers of categorisation and non identification of some pupils thereby placing an undue emphasis on within-child factors rather than full consideration of contextual factors.

Whiteshire had similar problems to *Mercia* with regard to cost containment and the LEA experienced an increase in statements from 4,100 to 10,000 during the period 1988 to 1998 (Table 6.4). Respondents in *Whiteshire* were also surprised about the lack of accountability from the LEA. As one Headteacher stated:

> I think it needs identifying for special needs ... yes otherwise I think there's a danger it's not used. I've always felt that the authority should have required schools to give a greater account of how they do spend that money. I think they've been rather remiss on that ... I mean nobody has ever checked up on me how we've spent it ... and I don't see why not. The authority has said we believe strongly in supporting special needs we are putting 6 point something percent of the budget towards that but nobody says tell me how you've spent it. (Whiteshire Headteacher)

Conclusions

This Chapter has examined the policy and practice of two LEAs which have different resourcing mechanisms for distributing their budgets for special educational needs. *Mercia*'s professional audit of needs which focuses on teaching arrangements, is generally welcomed by the professionals who were interviewed. However strong reservations were made about the high level of administrative time which was necessary to complete the assessment process. *Whiteshire* used educational testing information for distribution purposes. Although this is a simpler process respondents were critical about the unit resourcing costs which meant that all pupils who qualified for additional money received the same amount irrespective of the nature or degree of their need.

The purpose of additional funding for special educational needs will determine a number of further considerations. If the purpose is for equity reasons then the use of social disadvantage data collected at the school level, which is favoured by most LEAs, might be justified on the grounds that this readily available information is well correlated with educational achievement data (Sammons, 1991). However it is unclear from policy documents whether *Mercia* and *Whiteshire* have attempted to shift the focus to the purpose of raising educational achievement. In practice *Mercia's* professional audit uses data which is collected totally at the individual pupil level and *Whiteshire* uses both social disadvantage and educational test data in the primary sector and test information only in the secondary sector. Differential costs for varying levels and type of need only become an important issue when the amount of funding is perceived to be of significant value. In *Mercia* the funding for non-statemented special educational needs is generally not considered to be high and therefore respondents did not consider financial differentiation a priority. Table 6.2 shows the level of funding which was available for non-statemented SEN pupils. Although the funding was much higher in *Whiteshire,* it does not appear to have had an impact on the numbers of pupils with a statement of SEN.

Respondents from both LEAs were reluctant to quantify the resource levels which they felt were required by the pupils. The views of the SENCOs and the heads of department were undoubtedly shaped by historical provision. Understandably with the pressures of a full teaching schedule, few of them had thought in detail about some of the financial questions posed in this study. Their views are therefore recorded qualitatively i.e. more, ok, less resources required. The headteachers were in a better position to answer some of the more detailed financial questions but lacked the detailed individual pupil information. This information had been delegated to the SENCOs as suggested by the Code of Practice. If the amount of SEN funding which is received by the school is seen to be of significant value then it is perhaps worthwhile for the LEA to devise a method of differentiating financially between the levels of need. LEAs may consider to use the Code of Practice stages of assessment as a basis for funding pupils. This carries the inherent danger, already experienced in *Mercia*, of fuelling an inflation in the identification of pupils. As a consequence of LEAs working with finite budgets there would be a reduction in the unit costs for each stage or the need to apply more stringent criteria each year to reduce the numbers of identified pupils.

The evidence from the case studies indicates that there is no professional consensus about the level of resources required for the different 'types' of need or for the different levels of need (see also Crowther et al., 1998 and Dyson and Millward, 2002). It has shown that significant anomalies exist for the resource levels both thought to be required and currently designated for pupils of similar levels of learning difficulty even within the same authority. This finding may be a reflection of historical spending/funding by schools/LEAs as respondents appeared to be searching for a baseline of resourcing when considering their answers (see Wedell, 1983). A tension immediately exists for LEAs who are keen to match resources to the continuum of need. Allocating different resource levels to different types of need may reinforce 'categories' of learning difficulty. This is clearly against the spirit of the 1981 Education Act, and may not be beneficial to the overall educational needs of pupils. For example, the much higher level of identification for pupils experiencing specific learning difficulties in *Whiteshire* will have an impact on other educational sectors both within and outside the field of special educational need. Another tension exists over the funding of 'categories' of need as the study has also emphasised the general agreement that there is under-resourcing of pupils identified as experiencing emotional and/or behavioural difficulties. There are significant hidden pastoral costs in providing support for these pupils which ought to be allocated a sufficient level of resource. LEAs are therefore faced with a difficult dilemma. They will be criticised if they provide non differentiated unit costs for a whole range of special educational needs thereby following the 'school and teacher effectiveness' discourse. They will also be criticised if they attempt to provide a finely tuned system of resourcing which reinforces categories of need and places undue emphasis on within child variables rather than consideration of contextual variables (the 'special needs pupil' discourse).

Chapter Five has previously shown that some LEAs are keen to promote a method of resourcing which targets at the individual pupil level and are prepared to allocate an adequate level of funding which is set under the SEN budget heading. The implication of this policy is that it carries with it an element of accountability. It would seem reasonable, therefore for these LEAs to attempt to set up a differential funding mechanism albeit the lack of professional consensus about the level of resources required to meet special educational needs. Although *Mercia*'s professional audit uses individual pupil data, the LEA only provides £50 per pupil for additional and special educational needs, specifically under their non-statemented SEN budget headings and have perhaps justifiably kept to non differentiated resource levels but within bands. If LEAs do not see it as their role to monitor the use of SEN resources then it may be prudent for them to use the most simple of the resourcing mechanisms i.e. the use of free school meal data to generate a unitary cost. Governing bodies would then be charged with making the local decisions about the use of SEN resources and the onus for ensuring that the governing body renders accountability would rest with the parents. OFSTED inspection reports potentially provide information to parents on the amount and effectiveness of the SEN provision.

The study by Coopers and Lybrand (1996a) offers further insights into three conceptual models of SEN delivery: purchaser/provider; consortium and partnership. *Whiteshire* and *Mercia* illustrate more aspects of the purchaser/provider model rather than the consortium or partnership approaches. The Delegated Special Provision arrangements, now undertaken by both LEAs, is a good example of the purchaser/provider model. An example of the partnership model is the way in which LEAs and schools in partnership decide on the responsibility for SEN generally. This was not the case in *Mercia* and *Whiteshire* where the amounts allocated to non-statemented special educational needs seemed to be determined by historical arrangements and were not chosen by collective or joint agreement. There was no evidence in this case study of leadership from *Whiteshire* or *Mercia* to their schools. Both LEAs appeared to be very 'hands off' in terms of managerial style and left the responsibility directly to schools themselves (see Evans et al., 1995). This is perhaps understandable in the climate of maximum delegation and could be interpreted within the consortium context espoused by Coopers and Lybrand.

This Chapter has argued that the purpose and the accountability of the additional funding for special educational needs is paramount. It has provided evidence to answer Key Question 6 and has concluded that there does not appear to be a consistent professional view of resourcing. To Key Question 7 the conclusion is that financial differentiation is only a concern in an LEA where the level of funding for non-statemented SEN is set at a high level. Financial differentiation is a worthwhile consideration in *Whiteshire* as the AEN/SEN budget is comparatively high. However this study has been unable to provide suggestions as to how the differentiation should operate, due to the lack of a professional consensus about the resources required to meet varying levels of special educational needs.

Chapter 7

Summary and Conclusions

The issues surrounding the area of special educational needs and formula funding for inclusive education have been found in this book to be highly complex. This concluding Chapter will present the case that a well designed formula can be a key instrument of policy for Local Education Authorities (LEAs), especially within the areas of resource allocation and resource management. The first section will make reference to the aims and to the main points arising from the key questions. The second section will consider the theme of the relationship between research and policy making and assess the contribution of this research in relation to its policy making context.

Summary of the Main Points arising from the Aims and Key Questions

First Subsidiary Aim

Key Questions 1 to 3 map onto the first subsidiary aim of this book which is to investigate how the purposes underlying differential funding for special educational needs affect the rules or principles for allocation embodied in a funding formula (see again Table 1.1).

Key Question 1. How does the conceptualisation of special educational needs impact upon policy within Local Education Authorities?
Key Question 2. What contradictions and tensions are apparent when the purposes of providing additional funding for special educational needs are examined?
Key Question 3. What principles or criteria should be considered when evaluating a funding formula and how do they relate to the purpose of the additional funding?

A major theme of this book has been the conceptualisation of special educational needs presented as three policy discourse areas (Galloway,

Armstrong and Tomlinson, 1994). Galloway et al. contend that the 1988 Education Act was premised on the 'school failure' discourse whereby the 'problem' was seen as poor teaching and outdated ideology. Following the general elections in 1997 and 2001 and there was an opportunity for the new Labour governments to change the previous stance in the White Papers *Excellence in Schools* (DfEE, 1997a) and *Schools Achieving Success* (DfES, 2001e). However the 'school failure' discourse appears to be have been followed in both instances (e.g. Hattersley, 1997).

At an individual LEA level, Galloway et al.'s first two policy discourses are the most important and it should be borne in mind that they are not mutually exclusive. Local Management of Schools and Fair Funding with its emphasis on age weighted pupil units, and the Code of Practice which emphasis the importance of individual education plans, have both reinforced the notion of 'individualism' and have driven LEAs further towards the discourse of the special needs pupil. It could be argued that one strategy for raising school effectiveness is for teachers to be more aware of the learning needs and progress of pupils as individuals and to use assessment and recording systems to assist in this.

In general though I would support the policy drive by LEAs to move away from the special needs discourse and more towards the school and teacher effectiveness discourse, however this is unlikely to happen within the present legislation. Indeed with the increasing numbers of statements, individualism seems to be more entrenched than ever. The 1997 Green Paper *Excellence for all Children,* the subsequent Programme of Action and the revised 2001 Code of Practice, essentially build on the previous conceptualisations of special educational needs discussed in Chapter Two.

[The notion of individualism is given greater urgency when the purpose of providing additional resources is considered. It has been argued that the majority of LEAs are unclear about the definition of special educational needs and about the overlap between SEN and social deprivation.]Also as Dyson (2001) states, the decision making process whereby children receive different levels and forms of provision is neither transparent nor self-evidently rational.]

Two main purposes for providing additional resources have been examined i.e. to raise achievement and to compensate for social disadvantage. If an LEA considers that a focus on educational outcomes should be the main purpose, then the following considerations are important. Funds should be distributed to meet the needs of individual pupils thereby strengthening the hold of the 'special needs pupil' discourse. There should be differential costs for different SENs and there should be accountability of SEN resources. On the other hand if an LEA wishes to develop the 'school and teacher effectiveness' policy discourse and provide a focus on equity, then the use of an index of social disadvantage to fund schools might be justified on the grounds that this readily available information is well correlated with educational achievement data. Also policy makers may wish to deal with the issue of compensatory resourcing for social disadvantage, independently from low educational achievement.

The principles or criteria to be considered when evaluating a funding formula are scrutinised in Key Question 3 (Chapter Three). I shall now provide an example of how the principles relate to the AEN/SEN Index in *Whiteshire*, which has already been described in Chapter Six.

Table 7.1 Evaluation of Whiteshire's AEN/SEN Index

Principles	SEN Pupil Allocation	Social Disadvantage
Simplicity	3	3
Equity	2	2
Effectiveness	2	1
Responsiveness to Needs	1	1
Efficiency	1	3
Stability of Funding	3	3
Cost Containment	1	3
Accountability	1	1
Total	14	17

Note : 3 – criterion satisfied
2 – criterion partly satisfied
1 – criterion not satisfied

Table 7.1 illustrates a simple scoring system to assist in the evaluation. The present AEN/SEN Index in *Whiteshire* meets the criterion of simplicity in that the formulae can be readily understood and there is transparency about the source of the data which is used. The criterion of equity is a politically sensitive issue and also an extremely complex issue because of the different conceptions and definitions of equity (see Chapter Three). This principle is also important as the LEA's response to it will determine which policy discourse is emphasised and which is to be the main purpose of the additional funding. The purpose of *Whiteshire's* AEN/SEN Index is not documented but it is reasonable to assume that the LEA are concerned with educational outcomes as individual pupil attainment data are used, albeit at the school level. *Whiteshire's* AEN/SEN Index meets procedural equity in that there is a consistent application of agreed rules, it does not meet vertical equity as there is no differentiation of funding. *Whiteshire* use both educational test and social deprivation data. The sole use of social disadvantage data could present a dilemma for an LEA which wishes to follow the 'school and teacher effectiveness' policy discourse whilst also wishing to improve accountability.

With reference to the criterion of effectiveness, lack of LEA documentation in *Whiteshire* about the purpose of the additional funding under the AEN/SEN index, makes this difficult to evaluate. Also the principle of efficiency relates to the purpose of the resource allocation and to which policy discourse is followed. If compensation for social disadvantage is the main purpose then efficiency would not be as important as when the purpose is to raise educational achievement. This is because compensating for social disadvantage is only concerned with equity of inputs rather than emphasising the reduction of output differentials by raising educational achievement. *Whiteshire's* AEN/SEN Index can also be viewed as being inefficient as schools could affect the variables in the formula i.e. the educational attainment data, through their own actions. However the likelihood for schools to take this course of action is diminished since the publication of school performance data i.e. Key Stage 2 and GCSE results. A narrower definition of efficiency can be considered with respect to the amount of professional time required to collect the data required for inclusion in the formula. As the AEN/SEN Index uses group tests, this model is more efficient in terms of data collection than the professional audit approach used in *Mercia*.

Whiteshire put a high premium onto the principle of stability of funding. There is good stability of funding under the AEN/SEN Index as three year rolling averages are used. The principle of cost containment has been discussed in Chapter Three. *Whiteshire's* AEN/SEN Index does not appear to meet this criterion as there has been a considerable growth in the number of statements in *Whiteshire* (see Table 6.4). As mentioned in the Preface, the backcloth of this book has been the widespread concern about the escalating costs of providing for pupils with additional and special educational needs. However it is unreasonable to expect that a revised formula by itself will meet the criterion of cost containment. It is only one factor within a complex set of strategic choices faced by LEAs (Coopers and Lybrand, 1996a).

The principle of accountability is also not met by the AEN/SEN Index and this issue has already been discussed in Chapters Three and Six. This criterion becomes more important if an LEA pursues the 'special needs pupil' policy discourse. There is no expectation under the AEN/SEN funding arrangements in *Whiteshire* that schools should be held up to scrutiny about how they have used their resources allocated for additional educational needs. Despite the high priority placed upon raising standards and accountability by the White Papers *Excellence in Schools* (DfEE, 1997a) and *Schools Achieving Success* (DfES, 2001e), not all headteachers in *Whiteshire* are of the view that ring fencing of AEN/SEN funds should take place. An example of this view was received during a consultation about a revised AEN/SEN formula.

> The ring fencing of particular funds within the schools budget allocation is contrary to the philosophy of 'local management' of finances. It is essential in my view that schools maintain the greatest flexibility in the allocation of funds to particular budget headings if the variety of local needs and financing of particular projects are to be met (Headteacher Whiteshire).

Interestingly this comment was made by a Headteacher who was a member of the Secondary SEN Working Group as the representative of his teacher association. He presented the view that the formula should be more focussed towards funding at the individual pupil level rather than at the school level, but paradoxically, has also consistently pressed the LEA to provide more statements for pupils attending his school. This vignette is an example of an entrenched view about AEN/SEN funding which may be prevalent and enduring within *Whiteshire.* That is the view which encourages the LEA to release more centrally retained resources to meet the needs of individual pupils at School Action or School Action Plus whilst rejecting of the notion that there should be accountability. The view also motivates the school to extract more resources from the LEA by increasing the referral of pupils for section 323 statutory assessments. The challenge for the Authority, and indeed many other LEAs, is to change attitudes about the 'ownership' of SEN and for discussion and debate to take place about the respective responsibilities of the LEA and schools for pupils with AEN/SEN. The partnership model of SEN delivery (Coopers and Lybrand, 1996a) recognises the need to build a consensus and share responsibility with schools.

Second Subsidiary Aim

Key Questions 4 to 7 map onto the second subsidiary aim which is to examine the funding relationship between pupils with additional and special educational needs but without statements and pupils with statements in an attempt to develop a coherent approach to resourcing inclusive education throughout the continuum of SEN.

Key Question 4. What have been the historical arrangements for funding pupils with additional and special educational needs?

Key Question 5. What is the current practice in LEAs with regard to resource definition, resource allocation and resource management?

Key Question 6. What is the relationship between special educational needs and resource levels and how does this match professional views?

Key Question 7. Is it worthwhile for LEAs to differentiate financially between different levels of need?

As the second aim of the book is concerned with the funding relationship within the continuum of SEN, a full analysis of the background issues has been undertaken in Chapters Four to Six.

First, the historical arrangements for funding pupils with special educational needs and the legislative context within which formula funding operates have been considered in Chapter Four. In particular, Circular 11/90 (DES, 1990) has been examined, which offered long awaited guidance to LEAs about resource levels for pupils with statements of special educational needs and introduced the concept of the resource band of learning difficulty. However the impression should not be gained that resource bands are the panacea to resource management. There is the concern that resource bands may reinforce 'categories' of learning difficulty and place further emphasis on child variables rather than upon contextual variables. A further criticism is illustrated when the majority of pupils fall just 'inside' or 'outside' a band. Yet the advantages gained by differentiated funding, in terms of the potential of increased accountability and of the 'instant' resource allocation to those pupils in greatest need rather than having to wait for the lengthy completion of a statutory assessment, would seem to outweigh the disadvantages.

Second, the two EMIE surveys reported in Chapter Five (Marsh, 1997a, 2002), have looked at current practice in LEAs for resourcing additional and special educational needs. The surveys have provided an update of an earlier survey conducted by Lee (1992a). The first generation of AEN/SEN formulae made extensive use of free school meals (FSM) data as a means of predicting incidence levels of pupils with special educational needs. However there did not seem to be much enthusiasm about their continued use. This may have been related to the structures put into place by the Code of Practice which reinforces the discourse area of the 'special needs pupil', and a general movement by LEAs to a more needs led approach. It is more likely that the mistrust of FSM information is related to changes in demographic data and a reluctance by some families to register a claim.

There is also a widely held scepticism supported by research evidence, that a free school meals index, at a pupil level as opposed to the school level, is a poor predictor of learning difficulties. Despite these reservations the use of FSM by LEAs actually increased from 81 per cent in 1992 to 96 per cent in 2002. This may be partly due to the increasingly accepted use of FSM information, both as contextual data in OFSTED school inspection reports and for value added calculations in the Autumn Package (DfES, 2002b).

A high level of interest has been shown by LEAs in both EMIE surveys. This seems to be illustrative of the concern which exists about SEN budget levels generally and also of the willingness to pool ideas about the complexities surrounding the area. The distinct impression was gained throughout the surveys that education officers were keen to make sure that the benchmarking information and performance indicators obtained from their LEA, were within 'the normal range' and did not deviate too markedly from the 'mean'. This respect for the 'traditional approach' does not augur well for the radical reconceptualisation of special needs as proposed by Dyson and Gains (1993). The viewpoint has already been stated in Chapter Two that LEAs are continuing to focus on structures rather than a focus on processes. The research finding in Chapter Five would suggest that a conformity is sought with practice and policies adopted in most other LEAs, rather than an involvement in a deeper consideration of more general processes, for example an examination of the effectiveness of teaching approaches across the curriculum by the inspection/advisory teams within the LEA e.g. West et al., (1995).

Third, the case study conducted in two LEAs and reported in Chapter Six, examined the relationship between special educational needs (SEN) and resource levels and considered whether it is worthwhile for LEAs to differentiate financially between different levels of need. The conclusion to Key Question 6 was that there is no professional consensus about the level of resources required for different types of need or for different levels of need (see also Crowther et al., 1998, Dyson and Millward, 2002). The implication arising from this finding is that it is not worth the effort to devise a finely tuned points system which allocates resources for special educational needs as it is unlikely to find agreement and approval from teacher associations. On the other hand, provided that the level of funding for AEN/SEN is set at a high enough level, then the use of a differentiated broad banded approach may prove to be of value in the formula design to address the issues of vertical equity and responsiveness to needs.

In conclusion to the second aim of the book, the design of a coherent approach to resourcing throughout the continuum of SEN is an important issue and requires further development work by LEAs. The rapid changes in the funding arrangements for AEN/SEN has sharpened the focus for schools to examine their budgets far more closely than in previous eras. Under the arrangements in *Whiteshire* it is clearly in the schools best interests to promote as many pupils to statutory 323 assessments. It is not surprising therefore that the growth in the number of statements can be traced back to the introduction and implementation of LMS.

Whiteshire LEA wished to address this concern in future reviews by providing an enhanced level of support at School Action Plus in an attempt to stabilise the number of statements. It was felt that if schools were allocated differentiated funding for pupils close to the statementing threshold, then the motive for requesting a statement would be reduced.

If the 'SEN time bomb' is to be defused then an important step along the way will be the shaping of resource levels which improve the face validity of the AEN/SEN formula and narrow the resource gap between School Action Plus and for those pupils having a statement of special educational needs. This will only work if the allocation for having a statement is reduced and/or conversely if the allocation for a pupils at School Action Plus is markedly increased.

Policy Making and Research

The research reported in this book has been conducted following the significant policy impact of the 1988 Education Act which gave rise to the implementation of formula funding and Local Management of Schools in 1990. This section will now consider the interaction between policy making and this research and the impact which technical considerations could have in the development of any revised formula. The political and policy implications have always had a high profile in the book. I shall now consider models from Weiss' (1977) taxonomy, which have direct relevance to this book.

The first model is the classical *linear* model that has dominated the picture of how research is utilised in the physical sciences and postulates a chain from basic research to applied research to development and to application. This model also has similarities to the ideal model of rationalist decision-making (Simon, 1957) which includes as its features: a thorough analysis of current and future problems; involves the identification and then comprehensive evaluation of all policy options; and results in the adoption of solutions which are optimal given the values of the decision-making body (Hogwood and Gunn, 1984, p.45).

Weiss and most other commentators argue that the linear model is hardly applicable in the social sciences where 'knowledge does not readily lend itself to conversion into replicable technologies' (p.427). Likewise the rationalist model of decision making is of little use to those seeking a description of practice or even a feasible prescription for practice. As March (1978) argues, given current knowledge even so called 'rational choice' inherently involves a significant degree of guess-work, in particular 'guesses about future consequences of current actions and guesses about future preferences for those consequences'.

Weiss' first model, does not appear to be particularly apposite to this study because the assumptions do not apply. The work reported in this book does not have a basic research and applied research element and so does not meet the linear model criteria.

The second research model is the problem-solving one which postulates that specific studies are commissioned in order to assist pending policy decisions. This is considered by Weiss to be unrealistic on the grounds that policy makers do not, in fact, wait for what researchers have to tell them and then act on it, if only because there may be no consensus of goals between researchers and policy makers. This is particularly the case when the research suggests that more resources should be directed to a particular service or social problem.

A third type of research model is the interactive one where there is an assumption of no 'linearity' from research to utilisation but rather a 'disorderly set of inter-connections and back-and-forthness'. This model assumes the existence of dialogue between policy makers and researchers and has a likeness to the 'garbage-can' model of decision making (Cohen et al., 1972). The 'garbage-can' model assumes a fairly chaotic process in operation and that decision makers can and usually do operate without clearly defined goals.

The problem-solving and interactive models do apply rather well to studies in this area of research and postulate that specific studies are commissioned in order to assist pending policy decisions.

The fourth model is the *political* one which is also relevant to this research. What often happens is that a social issue after having been debated for some time has led to firm and entrenched positions that will not be shaken by new evidence. Research findings then become ammunition for one side in a policy dispute. Fulcher (1989) presents a good example of the *politics* in formulating policy in her account of the Review of Educational Services for the Disabled in Victoria, Australia. As she states:

> None of my previous work or personal experiences prepared me for the intensely political process involved in producing a report ... vigorous struggles

took place between Committee members and their associates in attempts to influence the Committee's decisions (p1).

An example of the *political model* occurred in one LEA where one teacher association (National Association of Schoolmasters/Union of Women Teachers, NAS/UWT) wanted an EBD component to be included in the formula to publicly acknowledge the perceived increase in behaviour difficulties experienced by schools. The increase in behaviour difficulties as measured by exclusion rates has been highlighted by a number of writers in recent years (e.g. Hayden, 1996; Parsons et al. 1997). The stance taken by the NAS/UWT has historical roots in the key role played by the NAS during the 1970s. The NAS actively campaigned to raise and pursue the issue of disruptive pupils in schools mainly in response to the Raising of the School Leaving Age (ROSLA) proposal, which was implemented in September 1972. Turkington (1986) has provided an in depth analysis of the coverage of deviance in schools by the educational press and has used the term 'the discovery of the disruptive pupil' to describe the emphasis of the 'special needs' discourse in the period after 1970. A more recent example of the emphasis of the 'special needs' discourse was the high profile taken by the NAS/UWT during the 1997 inspection of the Ridings school, in Calderdale LEA.

Other members on the working group in this LEA felt that to identify a formula element for Emotional and Behavioural Difficulties would place undue emphasis upon 'within child' factors rather than a full analysis of the school's behaviour policy, its ethos, organisation and curriculum, together with the teacher and their classroom management and teaching style. In other words the 'school and teacher effectiveness' discourse was being supported. The working group commissioned research to see whether there was any evidence to support the view that a correlation exists between low achievement and reported behavioural difficulties in pupils. The group considered the view that a formula element which reflects both social disadvantage and low achievement in schools may 'de facto' take account of likely incidence of behavioural difficulties perceived by schools. This research showed that a correlation does exist between schools with a high level of pupils in receipt of free school meals and reported numbers of pupils with behavioural difficulties (see Marsh, 1998). As the result did not support the line taken by the NAS/UWT, it is not surprising that the teacher association attempted to find fault with the research design.

Another example of how the research overlaps a further model from Weiss' taxonomy, is the tactical model. This model simply refers to the frequent tendency to 'bury' a controversial problem in research in order to have to defend procrastination or unwillingness to take immediate action.

The tactical model can also be compared with the incremental model of decision-making as a process of 'muddling through' (Lindblom, 1959), of policy-makers pursuing marginal changes to pre-existing policies, of viewing ends, means and values as inherently and reciprocally interrelated. The cynical observer might comment that this model could be the best fit of all if an LEA wanted to 'bury' a controversial problem.

The sixth is the enlightenment model which Weiss thinks is the one through which 'social science most frequently enters the policy arena'. All the research models make the assumption that the findings of a specific project are intended to, or should be, used to help make a specific policy decision. However Weiss argues that this is to misunderstand the nature of policy making. She contends that policy makers do not sit down to make a clearly defined decision, ponder various options, consider the relevant facts, including research findings, and then choose one of the options. In reality, policy making is less rational and more diffuse than this and research is only one of a number of competing and contradictory pressures that influence policy. Policy making itself is a constantly evolving long term process, involving many different actors who come and go. In a decentralised system it may not be clear where policy is made. The enlightenment model refers to the way research is 'permeating' the policy making process.

Much of the discussion in the book has centred on aspects of budget management and budgetary control as the research has been carried out against a national concern by Local Education Authorities that SEN budgets and the number of statements are continuing to rise (Marsh, 1997b). It has been argued that the AEN/SEN formula can play an important part in resource management and in policy making. Cost containment and the need to reduce and stabilise the rate of statementing are important criteria or principles by which the formula can be evaluated. If the number of statements continue to grow then the main implication for LEAs is that, within the context of finite budgets, these increases will exert pressure on other already stretched budgets areas and will impact upon the amount that LEAs are able to distribute for pupils with special educational needs but without statements. The growth in the number of statements in *Whiteshire* since 1988 is detailed in Table 6.4 (Chapter Six). Statements in *Whiteshire* increased by nearly 150 per cent from 1988 to 1998. There has also been a significant increase nationally, from 165,000 in 1992 to 265,000 statements in 2002 (a 60 per cent increase) (SEN2 surveys DfES, 2002c), although the evidence now suggests that the trend may be beginning to slow (Marsh, 2003 in press).

A number of other reports have referred to the growth in statements e.g. Audit Commission (1992a, 1992b, 1994, 2002a) and Coopers and Lybrand (1996a). These reports have recommended that means should be identified of redirecting resources from statemented to non-statemented provision, to promote early intervention and preventative work and so reducing the demand for a statement. A well designed and funded AEN/SEN formula can assist with the accountability of resources and can help to prevent a pupil requiring a statutory assessment thereby providing opportunities for the recycling of resources into School Action Plus.

The principle of maintaining a pupil at School Action Plus with additional resources provided by the school rather than providing the protection of a statement, is not universally accepted by all parties. The Independent Panel for Special Education Advice (IPSEA, 1997) has provided a strong criticism of *The SEN Initiative* (Coopers and Lybrand, 1996a) claiming that its recommendations will prejudice the legal right of children to receive the special educational provision their special educational needs calls for. IPSEA believe that large numbers of disabled children are not receiving the provision to which they are legally entitled and that *The SEN Initiative* has had a worsening effect. They have cited case law from two High Court judgements which has made explicit the LEAs' duty to arrange the special educational provision required to meet a child's special educational needs as specified in the statement. In R v Hillingdon London Borough Council, ex parte Governing Body of Queensmead School, 10th December 1996 the judgement confirmed that if a LEA's formula did not produce sufficient resources to meet the child's needs then the LEA would have to make up the balance and could not require a school to do so (The Times, 9th January 1997). In R v Harrow London Borough Council ex parte M, 8th October 1996, the judgement confirmed the right of LEAs to request other bodies (e.g. a Health Authority) to make the special educational provision a child required, but if that was not forthcoming, there was no 'let-out' for the authority, they must themselves arrange the special educational provision the child required. In the words of Mr Justice Turner:

... this duty is owed personally to the child and the duty is not by this section delegable.

Whilst the child advocacy actions of IPSEA can be interpreted as working for the best interests of the child, it does illustrate the negative aspects of the competitive market forces model whereby the 'educationally fittest' will survive at the expense of those who are less well informed or educated. Indeed yet more emphasis is placed on the confrontational aspects of attempting to extract statements and resources for the '2 per cent' of pupils whilst neglecting the needs of the '18 per cent'. Parents have been encouraged by previous Governments to behave as critical consumers in the market place seeking out the services they required and rejecting those which did not conform to their specifications. There is evidence (e.g. Riddell, 1994; Gross, 1996) that middle class parents have been successful in securing more of the type of education they require for their own children e.g. specific learning difficulties, and this will be at the expense of others who are less articulate. For example, the number of appeals registered by the SEN and Disability Tribunal has increased by 49 per cent over the five year period 1997 to 2002 (Marsh, 2003 in press). In particular the proportion of appeals registered by the Special Educational Needs Tribunal, where the main need was specific learning difficulties, have been in the range from 34 per cent to 40 per cent since the first appeal was heard in 1995. Riddell (1994) felt that because the competition is not a 'fair' one, market forces will not only maintain but increase educational inequalities. She argues that it is possible for a relatively powerful group of parents with the support of voluntary organisations, such as IPSEA, to shift the balance of resources in favour of their children. On the other hand it is also likely that articulate parents would accrue resources for their children at the expense of children from less articulate parents, even if there was no schools' market (i.e. pupils were allocated to schools by the LEA with no parental choice).

The principle of equity has already been shown to be an important criterion to be considered when evaluating a AEN/SEN formula. The pressure exerted by parents of children experiencing specific learning difficulties to secure resources, will severely test the equity principle. Despite the pressure, this book proposes that a well designed and well funded SEN formula can address aspects of procedural and distributional equity not only for pupils with general learning difficulties but also those experiencing SpLD. That is to say procedural equity would be satisfied by the consistent application of agreed rules rather than relying on previously flawed methods of allocation such as officer discretion. With respect to specific learning difficulties (SpLD) it has been argued that SpLD falls randomly across the population and therefore the argument to include a factor in an AEN/SEN formula addressing SpLD is all the more weaker. LEAs could make particular reference to the funding of SpLD by suggesting that the 'hidden 5 per cent' from the Age Weighted Pupil Unit element should be used for allocating resources to pupils experiencing specific learning difficulties analogous to the 'planned place' element of the Special Schools LMS formula. This argument highlights two previous issues i.e. the accountability of resources and whether the concept of the statement is still workable (see Williams and Maloney, 1998; Audit Commission, 2002a).

In conclusion, this research has set out to investigate the principles and practice for allocating resources to provide for pupils with additional and special educational needs (AEN/SEN) within the context of inclusive education. The book has been written against the backcloth of changing legislation and with numerous updating of government circulars. The enduring characteristic of recent years has been the increasing number of pupils with statements of SEN and the associated pressures on fiscal control, so inevitably much of the commentary has centred on issues of budget management. Evidence has been obtained throughout the study relating to the key questions set out in Chapter One, and consideration has been given to the principles necessary for the design of an 'improved' AEN/SEN formula.

There continues to be much interest in the area of educational finance and special educational needs. At the time of writing this conclusion the national consultation about options for changing the system of grant support for local authorities had just been completed. A new LEA funding system for education has been proposed to replace the Education Standard Spending Assessment, the final details were first announced on 5th December 2002 (Local Government Finance information is available from the Office of the Deputy Prime Minister's web page www.odpm.gov.uk). The Government originally set out its proposals for reforming funding for LEAs and schools in a Green Paper *Modernising Local Government Finance* (DETR, 2000). In addition, there has also been a major study published by the Audit Commission looking at how well children's needs are being met by local authorities in the context of the Government policy on inclusion (Audit Commission, 2002a, 2002b).

The Green Paper *Excellence for all Children* (DfEE, 1997b) proposed that as a result of improvements arising from the conclusions, then the proportion of children who need a statement will be moving towards 2 per cent. The latest Government statistics indicate that the percentage of statements has continued to increase, from 2.8 per cent in 1997 to 3.0 per cent in 2002 (DfES, 2002c). LEAs will be able to engage in the policy drive of early release of delegated resources for pupils with additional and special educational needs, only if the demand for statements can be reduced. Some LEAs, e.g. City of Southampton, have achieved this goal by setting the target of reducing the reliance on statements while promoting inclusion, with the specific policy of refocusing and recycling resources on more preventative work with schools, children and families.

It is clear from the latest EMIE survey (Marsh, 2002) that there continues to be importance given by LEAs to refining and reviewing their AEN/SEN funding formulae to support inclusive education. Clearly it is too simplistic to think that a revision of the funding formula and an increase in the budget allocation will automatically reduce the demand for statements and increase inclusion. In forthcoming debates about the continued use of delegated funding, the question of accountability and what is to be expected from schools' generally available provision, will continue to be paramount. Also the issues of participation, removing barriers, ownership and belonging are fundamental for future developments in inclusion. The challenge for LEAs and schools is to develop inclusive education policies and formula funding arrangements which fully encompass the needs of *all* pupils with additional and special educational needs.

Bibliography

ACE (1992) Exclusions *Advisory Centre for Education Bulletin* 45 (January).

Achilles, C.M., Nye, B.A., Zaharias, J.B., Fulton, D. and Bingham, S. (1993) *Prevention or Remediation? Is Small Class a Reasonable Treatment for Either?* Paper Given to National Conference of Professors of Educational Administration, Palm Springs, California.

Adams, F. (Ed) (1986) *Special Education.* Harlow: Councils and Education Press.

Ainscow. M. (1991a) Effective Schools For All: An Alternative Approach to Special Needs in Education. *Cambridge Journal of Education* 21 (3) pp 293-303.

Ainscow, M. (Ed) (1991b) *Effective Schools for All.* London: Fulton.

Ainscow, M. (1993) *Towards Effective Schools for All. Policy Options For the Special Educational Needs in the 1990s.* Stafford: NASEN.

Ainscow, M. and Muncey, J. (1989) *Meeting Individual Needs in the Primary School.* London: Fulton.

Armstrong, D. (1995) *Power and Partnership in Education : Parents, Children and Special Educational Needs.* London: Routledge.

Association of Metropolitan Authorities (AMA) (1995) *Partnership, Quality and Accountability.* London: AMA.

Audit Commission, (1985) *Audit Commission Handbook: A Guide to Economy, Efficiency and Effectiveness.* London: HMSO.

Audit Commission / HM Inspectorate (1992a) *Getting In On the Act. Provision For Pupils with Special Educational Needs.* London: HMSO.

Audit Commission / HM Inspectorate (1992b) *Getting the Act Together. Provision For Pupils with Special Educational Needs.* London: HMSO.

Audit Commission (1994) *The Act Moves On: Progress in Special Educational Needs.* London: HMSO.

Audit Commission (2000) *Money Matters School Funding and Resource Management.* London: Audit Commission.

Audit Commission / OFSTED (2002) *LEA Strategy for the Inclusion of Pupils with Special Educational Needs.* London: OFSTED.

Audit Commission (2002a) *Statutory assessment and statements of SEN: in need of review?* London: Audit Commission.

Audit Commission (2002b) *Special Educational Needs: A Mainstream Issue.* London: Audit Commission.

Bailey, T. (1989) A Positive Approach To the Education Reform Act. *Support For Learning* 4 (2) pp 75-82.

Barton, L. (1993) Labels, Markets and Inclusive Education, In J. Visser and G. Upton (Eds) *Special Education In Britain After Warnock*. London: David Fulton.

Baskind, S. and Thompson, D. (1995) Using Assistants to Support the Educational Needs of Pupils with Learning Difficulties: the Sublime or the Ridiculous? *Educational and Child Psychology* 12 (2) pp 46-57.

Bassey, M. (1995) When do the Numbers Get Too Great? *Times Educational Supplement* 12 May 1995 p 10.

Beek, C. (2002). The Distribution of resources to support inclusive learning. *Support for Learning* 17 (1) pp 9-14.

Bennett, N. (1991) The Quality of the Classroom Learning Experiences For Children With Special Educational Needs, In M. Ainscow (Ed) op.cit.

Bennett, N. (1996) Class Size In Primary Schools: Perceptions of Headteachers, Chairs of Governors, Teachers and Parents. *British Educational Research Journal* 22 (1) pp 33-55.

Berger, M., Yule, W. and Rutter, M. (1975) Attainment and Adjustment In Two Geographical Areas: (ii) the Prevalence of Specific Reading Retardation. *British Journal of Psychiatry*. 126 (5) pp 10-19.

Bernstein, B. (1970) Education Cannot Compensate for Society. *New Society* 387 pp 344-347.

Bibby, P. and Lunt, I. (1996) *Working For Children*. London: David Fulton.

Bickel, W.E. and Bickel, D.D. (1986) Effective Schools, Classrooms and Instruction: Implications For Special Education. *Exceptional Children* 52 (6) pp 489-500.

Bines, H. (1995) Special Educational Needs in the Market Place. *Journal of Education Policy* 10 (2) pp 157-171.

Bines, H. and Loxley, A. (1995) Implementing the Code of Practice for Special Educational Needs. *Oxford Review of Education* 21 (4) pp 381-393.

Blatchford, P. and Mortimore, P. (1994) the Issue of Class Size For Young Children In Schools: What Can We Learn From Research? *Oxford Review of Education* 20 (4) pp 411-428.

Board of Education (1931) *Report of the Consultative Committee On the Primary School*. London: HMSO.

Booth, T. (1994) Continua Or Chimera? *British Journal of Special Education* 21 (1) pp 21-24.

Brookhover, W., Beady, C., Flood. P., Schweitzer, J. and Wisenbaker, J. (1979) *School Social Systems and Student Achievement; Schools can make a Difference*. New York: Praeger.

Brophy, J.E. (1983) Classroom Organisation and Management. *The Elementary School Journal* 82 pp 266-285.

Brown, M. (1989) Graded Assessment and Learning Hierarchies In Mathematics, An Alternative View. *British Educational Research Journal* 15 pp 121-128.

Burstall, C. (1992) Playing the Numbers Game in Class. *Education Guardian* 7 April p 23.

Burt, C. (1937) *The Backward Child*. London: University of London Press.

Cambridgeshire County Council (1993) *Activity Led Staffing*. Education Committee Report, 12 October 1993.

Central Advisory Council for Education (CACE) (1967) *Children and their Primary Schools*. (The Plowden Report) London: HMSO.

Centre for Studies on Inclusive Education (CSIE) (2001) *Money for Inclusion*. Third Edition, June 2001. Bristol: CSIE.

Cohen, D. March, J., and Olsen, J. (1972) A Garbage-Can Model of Organisational Change. *Administrative Science Quarterly* 17 (1)

Coleman, J.S., Campbell, E., Hobson, C., McPartland, J., Mood, A., Weinfield, F. and York, R. (1966) *Equality of Educational Opportunity*. Washington: National Center For Educational Statistics.

Coopers and Lybrand (1996a) *the SEN Initiative – Managing Budgets For Pupils with Special Educational Needs*. London: Coopers and Lybrand.

Coopers and Lybrand (1996b) *the Funding of Education*. Report Commissioned By the National Union of Teachers. London: NUT.

Corwin, R.G. and Kerckhoff, A.C. (1981) *Research In Sociology of Education and Socialisation: A Research Annual*, Vol. 2. Greenwich: Research On Educational Organisations.

Croll, P. and Moses, D. (1985) *One In Five: the Assessment and Incidence of Special Educational Needs*. London: Routledge.

Crowther, D., Dyson, A. and Millward, A. (1998) *Costs and Outcomes for Pupils with Moderate Learning Difficulties in Special and Mainstream Schools*. RR89. London: DfEE.

Davie, R., Butler, N. and Goldstein, H. (1972) *From Birth To Seven*. London: Longman/National Children's Bureau.

Department of Education and Science (1965) *Circular 10/65 the Organisation of Secondary Education*. London: DES.

Department of Education and Science (1973) *Circular 4/73 Staffing of Special Schools and Classes*. London: DES.

Department of Education and Science (DES) (1978) *Report of the Committee of Enquiry into Special Educational Needs*. (The Warnock Report). London: HMSO.

Department of Education and Science (DES) (1981) *Circular 8/81 The Education Act 1981*. London: DES

Department of Education and Science (DES) (1983) *Circular 1/83 Assessments and Statements of Special Educational Needs*. (Joint Circular with DHSS Health Circular (83)3 and Local Authority Circular LAC (83)2). London: DES.

Department of Education and Science (DES) (1985) *Education For All* (The Swann Report). London: HMSO.

Department of Education and Science (DES) (1988a) *Circular 7/88 Education Reform Act: Local Management of Schools*. London: DES.

Department of Education and Science (DES) (1988b) *Task Group on Assessment and Testing: A Report*. London: HMSO.

Department of Education and Science (DES) (1989a) *Circular 22/89 Assessments and Statements of Special Educational Needs: Procedures within the Education, Health and Social Services.* London: DES.

Department of Education and Science (DES) (1989b) *Discipline In Schools.*(Elton Report). HMSO: London

Department of Education and Science (DES) (1990) Circular *11/90 Staffing for Pupils with Special Educational Needs.* London: DES.

Department of Education and Science (DES) (1991) *Circular 7/91Local Management of Schools: Further Guidance.* London: DES.

Department for Education (DfE) (1992a) *Consultation Document 1. A Common Funding Formula for Grant Maintained Schools.* London: DfE.

Department for Education (DfE) (1992b) *Public Examination Results.* London: DfE.

Department for Education (DfE) (1993a) *Consultation Document 2. A Common Funding Formula for Grant-Maintained Schools.* London: DfE.

Department for Education (DfE) (1993b) *Local Management of Schools and Pupils with Special Educational Needs. A Report by HMI.* London: DfE.

Department for Education (DfE) (1993c) *Education for Disaffected Pupils, 1990-1992. Ofsted Report.* London: HMSO.

Department for Education (DfE) (1994a) *Code of Practice on the Identification and Assessment of Special Educational Needs.* London: DfE.

Department for Education (DfE) (1994b) *Circular 2/94 Local Management of Schools.* London: DfE.

Department for Education (DfE) (1995) *The National Curriculum.* London: DfE.

Department for Education and Employment (DfEE) (1997a) *Excellence in Schools.* White Paper. London: DfEE.

Department for Education and Employment (DfEE) (1997b) *Excellence for All Children.* Green Paper. London: DfEE.

Department for Education and Employment (DfEE) (1998a) *Meeting Special Educational Needs – A Programme of Action.* London: DfEE.

Department for Education and Employment (DfEE) (1998b) *Fair Funding: Improving Delegation to Schools. Consultation Paper.* London: DfEE.

Department for Education and Employment (DfEE) (2001a) *Supporting the Target Setting Process.* London: DfEE. (available from www.dfes.gov.uk/sen)

Department for Education and Skills (2001b). *The Distribution of Resources to Support Inclusion* (Guidance to LEAs), London: DfES

Department for Education and Skills (2001c). *Special Educational Needs Code of Practice.* London: DfES.

Department for Education and Skills (2001d). *Inclusive Schooling Children with Special Educational Needs* Statutory Guidance. London: DfES.

Department for Education and Skills (2001e). *Schools Achieving Success.* White Paper. London: DfES.

Department for Education and Skills (DfES) (2002a) *Statistics First Release 10/2002 Permanent Exclusions from Schools and Exclusion Appeals, England 2000/01.* London: DfES.

Department for Education and Skills (DfES) (2002b) *Autumn Package of Pupil Performance Information.* London: DfES.

Department for Education and Skills (DfES) (2002c) *Statistics of Education: Special Educational Needs in England, January 2002. DfES Statistical Bulletin. Issue No 10/02 November 2002.* London: DfES.

Department of the Environment, Transport and the Regions (2000) *Modernising Local Government Finance.* A Green Paper. London: DETR.

Dessent, T. (1987) *Making the Ordinary School Special.* Lewes: Falmer Press.

Downes, P. (1993) Overspending ? Over-Funding. *Managing Schools Today* 3 (1) pp 4-7

Dyson, A. (2001) Special Needs Education as the way to equity: an alternative approach? *Support for Learning* 16 (3) pp 99-104.

Dyson, A. and Gains, C. (Ed.) (1993) *Rethinking Special Needs In Mainstream Schools Towards the Year 2000.* London: David Fulton.

Dyson, A., Millward, A. and Skidmore, D. (1994) Beyond the Whole School Approach: An Emerging Model of Special Needs Practice and Provision In Mainstream Secondary Schools. *British Educational Research Journal* 20 (3) pp 301-317.

Dyson , A. and Millward, A. (2002) *Decision – Making and Provision within the Framework of the SEN Code of Practice.* RR248. London: DfES.

Easterby-Smith, M., Thorpe, R. and Lowe, A. (1994) Analysing Qualitative Data, In N. Bennett, R. Glatter and R. Levačić (Eds) *Improving Educational Management Through Research and Consultancy.* London: Paul Chapman.

Edmonds, R. (1982) Programs of School Improvement: An Overview. *Educational Leadership* 40 (3) pp 4-11.

Evans, J. and Lunt, I. (1990) *Local Management of Schools and Special Educational Needs.* A Report of a Conference. February 1990. London: Institute of Education.

Evans, J., Lunt, I., Young, P. and Vincent, C. (1994) *Local Management of Schools and Special Educational Needs.* Final Report to the ESRC.

Evans, J., Castle, F. and Cullen, M.A. (2001) *Fair Funding? LEA policies and methods for funding additional and special needs – and schools' responses.* Slough: NFER.

Feiler, A. and Thomas, C. (1988) Special Needs: Past, Present and Future, In G. Thomas and A. Feiler (Eds) *Planning and Provision For Special Needs.* Oxford: Blackwell.

Fish, J. (1989) *What is Special Education?* Milton Keynes: Open University Press.

Fish, J. and Evans, J. (1995) *Managing Special Education.* Buckingham: Open University Press.

Fitz-Gibbon, C. T. (1996) *Monitoring Education. Indicators, Quality and Effectiveness.* London: Cassell.

Fletcher-Campbell, F. (1996) *the Resourcing of Special Educational Needs.* Slough: National Foundation for Educational Research (NFER).

Fletcher, J., Shaywitz, S., Shankweiler, D., Katz, L., Liberman, I., Stuebing, K., Francis, D., Fowler, A. and Shaywitz, B. (1994) Cognitive Profiles of Reading

Disability: Comparisons of Discrepancy and Low Achievement Definitions. *Journal of Educational Psychology* 86 (1) pp 6-23.

Fogelman, K. (Ed) (1976) *Britain's 16 Year Olds.* London: National Children's Bureau.

Fulcher, G. (1989) *Disabling Policies? A Comparative Approach To Education Policy and Disability.* London: Falmer Press

Galloway, D. (1985) *Schools, Pupils and Special Educational Needs.* London: Croom Helm.

Galloway, D., Armstrong, D. and Tomlinson, S. (1994) The *Assessment of Special Educational Needs: Whose Problem?* Harlow: Longman.

Gipps, C., Goldstein, H. and Gross, H. (1985) Twenty Per Cent With Special Needs: Another Legacy From Cyril Burt? *Remedial Education* 20 (2) pp72-75.

Goacher, B., Evans, J., Welton, J. and Wedell, K. (1988) *Policy and Provision for Special Educational Needs.* London: Cassell.

Gray, P. and Dessent, T. (1993) Getting Our Act Together. *British Journal of Special Education* 20 (1) pp 9-11.

Gross, J. (1996) The Weight of the Evidence: Parental Advocacy and Resource Allocation To Children With Statements of Special Educational Need. *Support For Learning* 11 (1) pp 3-8.

Gross, J (2000) Paper promises? Making the Code work for you. *Support for Learning* 15 (3) pp 126-133.

Hamilton, D. (1995) Peddling Feel-Good Fictions. *Forum* 38 (2) pp 54-56.

Hargreaves, D.H. (1982) *The Challenge of the Comprehensive School : Culture, Curriculum, Community.* London: Routledge and Kegan Paul.

Hattersley, R. (1997) Comparisons are Otiose, *Times Educational Supplement* 15 August.

Hayden, C. (1996*) Exclusive Education Annual Report 1995-96, In Economic and Social Research Council Annual Report.* Swindon: ESRC.

Hill, D., Oakley-Smith, B and Spinks, J. (1990) *Local Management of Schools.* London: Paul Chapman Publishing.

Hill, P.W. and Ross, K.N. (1999) Issues In Funding Pupil Specific Factors Related To Supplementary Educational Need, In K. Ross and R. Levačić (Eds) *Needs Based Resource Allocation In Education By Formula Funding of Schools.* Paris: International Institute for Educational Planning.

Hodgetts, C. (1995) Sizing Up the Classroom. *Times Educational Supplement* 12 May p 14.

Hogwood, B. and Gunn, L. (1984) *Policy Analysis for the Real World.* Oxford: Oxford University Press.

Housden, P. (1992) *Bucking the Market: LEAS and Special Needs.* Stafford: National Association for Special Educational Needs (NASEN).

House of Commons Education Committee (1993) *Third Report. Meeting Special Educational Needs: Statements of Need and Provision.* Volume II. London: HMSO.

House of Commons Education Committee (1994) *First Report. A Common Funding Formula for Grant-Maintained Schools.* London: HMSO.

House of Commons Education Committee (1996) *Special Educational Needs: the Working of the Code of Practice and the Tribunal.* Second Report. London: HMSO.

Hutchison, D. (1993) School Effectiveness Studies Using Administrative Data. *Educational Research* 35 (1) pp 27-47.

Independent Panel for Special Education Advice (IPSEA) (1997) *Briefing on the SEN Initiative.* Unpublished Paper. Woodbridge, Suffolk: IPSEA.

Inner London Education Committee (1974) *Education Committee Minutes of 17 September.*

Inner London Education Authority (1985) *Educational Opportunities for All,* The Fish Report. London: ILEA.

Jencks, C.S., Smith, M., Ackland, H., Bane, M.J., Cohen, D., Gintis, H., Heyns, B. and Micholson, S. (1972) *Inequality: A Reassessment of the Effect of Family and Schooling in America.* New York: Basic Books.

Jessen, D. and Gray, J. (1991) Slants on Slopes: Using Multi-Level Models To Investigate Differential School Effectiveness and its Impact on Pupils' Examination Results. *School Effectiveness and School Improvement* 2 (3) pp 230-271.

Jones, N. (1982) Children with Special Educational Needs: The Legislative Framework, in J. Welton et al. *Meeting Special Educational Needs: The 1981 Act and its Implications.* Bedford Way Paper No 12. London: Heinemann.

Jowett, S., Fletcher-Campbell, F., Evans, C. and Lee, B. (1996) *The Implementation of the Code of Practice on the Identification and Assessment of Special Educational Needs.* Interim Report. Slough: NFER.

Knight, B. (1993a) *Financial Management For School.* London: Heinemann.

Knight, R. (1993b) *Special Educational Needs and the Application of Resources.* Slough: EMIE.

Le Grand, J. (1991) Equity *and Choice: An Essay in Applied Social Policy.* London: Harper Collins.

Le Grand, J. and Bartlett, W. (1993) (Eds) *Quasi-Markets and Social Policy.* Basingstoke: Macmillan.

Lee, T. (1992a) *Additional Educational Needs and LMS: Methods and Money 1992-3.*Unpublished Paper. University of Bath.

Lee, T. (1992b) Finding Simple Answers To Complex Questions : Funding Special Needs Under LMS, In G. Wallace *Local Management of Schools : Research and Experience.* BERA Dialogues No 6. Clevedon: Multilingual Matters Ltd.

Lee, T. (1992c) Local Management of Schools and Special Education, In T. Booth, W. Swann, M. Masterton and P. Potts *Learning For All 2: Policies For Diversity in Education.* London: Routledge.

Lee, T. (1995) *The Search For Equity.* PhD Thesis. University of Bath.

Lee, T. (1996) *The Search For Equity. The Funding of Additional Educational Needs Under LMS.* Aldershot: Avebury.

Lewis, A. (1995) Policy Shifts Concerning Special Educational Provision in Mainstream Primary Schools. *British Journal of Educational Studies* 43 (3) pp 318-332.

Levačić, R. (1989) Formula Funding For Schools and Colleges, in R. Levačić (Ed.) *Financial Management In Education.* Milton Keynes: Open University Press.

Levačić, R. (1992) Local Management of Schools: Aims, Scope and Impact. *Educational Management and Administration* 20 (1) pp 16-29.

Levačić, R. (1993) Assessing the impact of formula funding in schools. *Oxford Review of Education* 19 (4) pp 435-457.

Levačić, R. (1995) *Local Management of Schools.* Buckingham: Open University Press.

Lindblom, C. (1959) The Science of Muddling Through. *Public Administration Review* 19

LMS Initiative (1992) *Local Management of Schools: A Study into Formula Funding and Management Issues.* London: LMS Initiative

Lodge, P. and Blackstone, T. (1982) *Educational Policy and Educational Inequality.* Oxford: Martin Robertson.

Lorenz, S. (1992) Supporting Special Needs Assistants in Mainstream Schools. *Educational and Child Psychology* 9 (4) pp 25-33.

Lowe Boyd, W. (1992) the Power of Paradigms: Reconceptualising Educational Policy and Management. *Education Administration Quarterly* 28 (4) pp 504-528.

Lunt, I. and Evans, J. (1994) *Allocating Resources For Special Educational Needs Provision.* Seminar Paper 4.Stafford: National Association of Special Educational Needs (NASEN).

McConville, R., Booker, J., Davies, K. and Ross, A. (1990) *Indicators of Special Educational Needs.* LEA: Nottinghamshire.

March, J. (1978) Bounded Rationality, Ambiguity and the Engineering of Choice. *The Bell Journal of Economics* 9 (2)

Marsh, A.J. (1995a) The Effect on School Budgets of Different Non-Statemented Special Educational Needs Indicators within a Common Funding Formula. *British Educational Research Journal* 21(1) pp 99-115.

Marsh, A.J. (1996) *Criteria of Need. A Survey of Local Authority Policies and Practice.* Manchester: Society of Education Officers (Special Needs Standing Committee).

Marsh, A.J. (1997a) *Current Practice For Resourcing Additional Educational Needs In Local Education Authorities.* Slough: EMIE/NFER.

Marsh, A.J. (1997b) Pupils With Statements Set to Double. *Special Children,* May Issue 102 pp 11-12.

Marsh, A.J. (1997c) SEN Funding: SATs Data Could Help Out. *Managing Schools Today* 7 (2) pp 4-5.

Marsh, A.J. (1998) *Formula Funding and Special Educational Needs.* Unpublished PhD thesis. Milton Keynes: Open University.

Marsh, A.J. (1999) Two and Two Together. *Special Children* 116 (January) pp 19-20.

Marsh, A.J. (2000) Resourcing the Continuum of Special Educational Needs in Two LEAs. *Educational Management and Administration* 28 (1) pp 77-88.

Marsh, A.J. (2002) *Resourcing Additional and Special Educational Needs in England 10 Years On (1992-2002)*. Slough: EMIE/NFER. (available from www.nfer.ac.uk./emie).

Marsh, A.J. (2003 in press) On the Right Track. *Special Children* (April/May issue)

Millward, A. and Skidmore, D. (1995) *Local Authorities' Management of Special Needs*. York: Joseph Rowntree Foundation.

Ministry of Education (1946) *Special Educational Treatment*. Pamphlet No 5. London: HMSO.

Ministry of Education (1959a) *The Handicapped Pupils and Special Schools Regulations*. London: HMSO.

Ministry of Education (1959b) *Primary Education: Suggestions for the Consideration of Teachers and Others Concerned with the Work of the Primary Schools*. London: HMSO.

Ministry of Education (1963) *Half Our Future*. London: HMSO.

Monk, D. (1990) *Educational Finance: An Economic Approach*. New York: McGraw Hill.

Mortimore, P., Sammons, P., Stoll, L., Lewis. D. and Ecob, R. (1988) *School Matters : The Junior Years*. Wells: Open Books.

Mortimore, P. and Blatchford, P. (1993) *The Issue of Class Size*. National Commission on Education Briefing Paper No. 12. March 1993.

National Curriculum Council (NCC) (1989) *Curriculum Guidance 2. A Curriculum for All. Special Educational Needs in the National Curriculum*. York: NCC.

National Union of Teachers (NUT) (1992) *NUT Survey on Pupils' Exclusions: Information from LEAs*. NUT Report. June.

Norgate, R. (1995) High Dependency: An Objective Framework for Staffing Schools for Children with Severe Learning Difficulties. *Educational Psychology in Practice* 10 (4) pp 247-256.

Norwich, B. (1994) *Segregation and Inclusion. English LEA Statistics 1988-1992*. Bristol: Centre for Studies on Inclusive Education (CSIE).

Norwich, B. (2002) *LEA Inclusion trends in England 1997-2001*. Bristol: Centre for Studies on Inclusive Education (CSIE).

Norwich, B., Evans, J., Lunt, I., Steedman, J. and Wedell, K. (1994) Clusters: Inter-School Collaboration in Meeting Special Educational Needs in Ordinary Schools. *British Educational Research Journal* 20 (3) pp 279-291.

Noss, R., Goldstein, H. and Hayes, C. (1989) Graded Assessment Learning Hierarchies In Mathematics. *British Educational Research Journal* 15 pp 109-120.

Nuttall, D., Goldstein, H., Prosser, R. and Rabash, H. (1989) Differential School Effectiveness. *International Journal of Educational Research* 13 (10) pp 769-776.

Nye, B.A., Achilles, C.A., Zaharias, J.B., Fulton, B.D. and Wallenhorst, M.P. (1992) *Small Is Far Better*. Paper Presented At Mid-South Educational Research Association, Knoxville, Tennessee.

Office for Standards in Education (Ofsted) (1993) Access *and Achievement in Urban Education*. London: HMSO.

Office for Standards in Education (Ofsted) (1995a) *Class Size and the Quality of Education.* London: Ofsted.

Office for Standards in Education (Ofsted) (1995b) *Guidance on the Inspection of Nursery and Primary Schools* London: HMSO.

Office for Standards in Education (Ofsted) (1995c) *Guidance on the Inspection of Secondary Schools* London: HMSO.

Office for Standards in Education (Ofsted) (1995d) *Guidance on the Inspection of Special Schools* London: HMSO.

Office for Standards in Education (Ofsted) (1996) *Promoting High Achievement for Pupils with Special Educational Needs.* London: HMSO.

Office for Standards in Education (Ofsted) (1997) *The SEN Code of Practice: Two years on.* London: HMSO.

Office for Standards in Education (Ofsted) (1999a) *The SEN Code of Practice: Three years on.* London: HMSO.

Office for Standards in Education (Ofsted) (1999b) *Inspecting Schools. The Framework.* London: Ofsted.

Organisation For Economic and Cultural Development (OECD) (1992) *Education at a Glance.* Paris: OECD.

Parsons, C., Castle, F., Howlett, K. and Worrall, J. (1997) *Exclusion from School: The Public Cost.* London: Commission for Racial Equality.

Porter, A.C. and Brophy, J.E. (1988) Synthesis of Research on Good Teaching: Insights From the Work of the Institute of Research On Teaching. *Educational Leadership* 48 (8) pp 74-85.

Pringle, M.L.K., Butler, N. and Davie, R. (1966) *11,000 Seven Year Olds.* London: Longman.

Pritchard, D.G. (1963) *Education and the Handicapped 1760-1960.* London: Routledge and Kegan Paul.

Purkey, S. and Smith, M. (1983) Effective Schools : A Review. *The Elementary School Journal* 83 (4) pp 427-452.

Reynolds, D. (1990) An Introduction to Managing School Effectiveness *School Organisation* 10 (2&3) pp 163-165.

Reynolds, D. (1995) School Effectiveness *Times Educational Supplement* 16 September 1995.

Riddell, S., Brown, S. and Duffield, J. (1994) Parental Power and Special Educational Needs: the Case of Specific Learning Difficulties. *British Educational Research Journal* 20 (3) pp 327-344.

Roaf, C. and Bines, H. (1989) Needs, Rights and Opportunities in Special Education, in C. Roaf and H. Bines (Eds) Needs, *Rights and Opportunities.* London: Falmer Press.

Robertson, A. (1995) *Survey of Funding Arrangements for Non-Statemented Special Educational Needs in England and Wales.* Middlesbrough: Cleveland County Council Education Department.

Rosenshine, B. (1971) *Teaching Behaviours and Student Achievement.* London: NFER.

Rosenshine, B. (1983) Teaching Functions in Instructional Programs. *The Elementary School Journal* 83 (4) pp 335-351.

Ross, K.N. (1983) *School Area Indicators of Educational Need.* Camberwell, Victoria: Australian Council for Educational Research.

Ross, K.N. and Levačić, R. (Eds) (1999) *Needs Based Resource Allocation In Education By Formula Funding of Schools.* Paris: International Institute for Educational Planning.

Rowan, P. (1988) Cause for Concern. *Times Educational Supplement* 29 July.

Rutter, M., Tizard, J. and Whitmore, K. (1970) *Education, Health and Behaviour.* London: Longman.

Rutter, M., Cox, A., Tupling, C., Berger, M. and Yule, W. (1975) Attainment and Adjustment in Two Geographical Areas: I The Prevalence of Psychiatric Disorder. *British Journal of Psychiatry.* 126 pp 493-509.

Rutter, M., Maughan, B., Mortimore, P. and Ouston, J. (1979) *Fifteen Thousand Hours : Secondary Schools and Their Effects on Children.* Wells: Open Books.

Sammons, P. (1992) *Measuring and Resourcing Educational Needs Variations in Leas' LMS Policies in Inner London.* Clare Market Paper Number 6. Centre For Educational Research: London School of Economics, University of London.

Sammons, P. (1996) Complexities In the Judgement of School Performance. *Educational Research and Evaluation* 2 (2) pp 113-149.

Sammons, P., Kysel, F. and Mortimore, P. (1983) Educational Priority Indices – A New Perspective. *British Educational Research Journal* 9 (1) pp 27-40.

Sammons, P., Nuttall, D.L. and Cuttance, P. (1993) Differential School Effectiveness : Results From A Reanalysis of the Inner London Education Authority's Junior School Project Data. *British Educational Research Journal* 19 (4) pp 381-405.

Sammons, P., Thomas, S., Mortimore, P., Owen, C. and Pennell, H. (1994) *Assessing School Effectiveness – Developing Measures to put School Performance in Context.* A Report by the Institute of Education for the Office for Standards in Education. London: University of London.

Sammons, P., Hillman, J. and Mortimore, P. (1995) *Key Characteristics of Effective Schools: A Review of School Effectiveness Research.* Report Commissioned by the Office of Standards in Education. London: Institute of Education and Office for Standards in Education.

School Examinations and Assessment Council (SEAC) (1992) *National Curriculum Assessment At Key Stage 1. 1992 Evaluation. Children with Statements of Special Educational Needs.* London: SEAC.

Scottish Education Department (SED) (1978) *The Education of Pupils with Learning Difficulties in Primary and Secondary Schools: A Progress Report by Her Majesty's Inspectorate.* Edinburgh: HMSO.

Shapson, S.M., Wright, E.N., Eason, G. and Fitzgerald, J. (1980) An Experimental Study of Class Size. *American Educational Research Journal* 65 pp 107-112.

Silver, H. and Silver, P. (1991) *An Educational War on Poverty. American and British Policy-Making 1960-1980.* Cambridge: Cambridge University Press.

Simkins, T. (1994) Efficiency, Effectiveness and the Local Management of Schools. *Journal of Education Policy* 9 (1) pp 15-33.

Simkins, T. (1995) the Equity Consequences of Educational Reform. *Educational Management and Administration* 23 (4) pp 221-232.

Simon, H. (1957) *Administrative Behaviour.* Toronto: Collier Macmillan.

Simpson, E. (1987) *Review of Curriculum-Based Staffing.* Slough: EMIE/NFER.

Slavin, R.E. (1989) Class Size and Student Achievement: Small Effects of Small Classes. *Educational Psychologist* 24 (1) pp 99-110.

Smith, G. (1987) Whatever Happened to Educational Priority Areas? *Oxford Review of Education* 13(1) pp 23-28.

Smith, D.J. and Tomlinson, S. (1989) *The School Effect: A Study of Multiracial Comprehensives.* London: Routledge.

Spalding, B. and Florek, A. (1989) Narrower Focus, Narrower Chances? *British Journal of Special Education* 16 (1) p 10.

Special Education Expenditure Project (SEEP) (2002) *What are we Spending on Special Education in the United States, 1999-2000?* Report submitted to United States Department of Education, Office of Special Education Programs. (www.seep.org)

Staffordshire County Council (1995) *Resource Review: The LMS Formula in the Light of the Evidence.* 17 July 1995.

Stanovich, K. (1994) Annotation: Does Dyslexia Exist? *Journal of Child Psychology and Psychiatry* 35 (4) pp 579-595.

Stanovich, K. and Siegal, L. (1994) Phenotypic Performance Profile of Children With Reading Disabilities: A Regression-Based Test of Phonological-Core Variable Difference Model. *Journal of Educational Psychology* 35 (4) pp 579-595.

Stewart, M. (1992) Local Management-the Kent Scheme, In G. Wallace *Local Management of Schools–Research and Experience.* BERA Dialogues No 6. Clevedon: Multilingual Matters.

Stoll, L. and Mortimore, P. (1995) *School Effectiveness and School Improvement.* Viewpoint No 2. London: Institute of Education, University of London.

Stoll, L. (1991) School Effectiveness in Action: Supporting Growth in Schools and Classrooms, in M. Ainscow (Ed) *Effective Schools for All.* London: Fulton.

Swann, W. (1992) Hardening the Hierarchies – The National Curriculum as a System of Classification, in T. Booth, W. Swann, M. Masterton and P. Potts (Eds) *Learning for All 1:Policies for Diversity in Education.* London: Routledge/Open University.

Tomlinson, T. (1990) Class Size and Public Policy: The Plot Thickens. *Contemporary Education* 62 (1) pp 17-23.

Touche Ross (1990) *Extending Local Management of Schools to Special Schools. A Feasibility Study for the Department of Education and Science.* London: Touche Ross.

Turkington, R.W. (1986) *In Search of the Disruptive Pupil. Problem Behaviour In Secondary Schools 1959-1982.* Unpublished PhD. Department of Sociology: University of Leeds.

Upton, G. (1992) No Time for Complacency. *Special Children* (July) pp23-27

Villette, S. (1993) *Weighting For Special Needs.* Paper Delivered at National LMS Seminar, Liverpool.

Vincent, C., Evans, J., Lunt, I . and Young, P. (1994) The Market Forces? The Effect of Local Management of Schools on Special Educational Needs Provision. *British Educational Research Journal* 20 (3) pp 261-277.

Vincent, C., Evans, J., Lunt, I. and Young, P. (1995) Policy and Practice : The Changing Nature of Special Educational Needs Provision in Schools. *British Journal of Special Education* 22 (1) pp 4-11.

Wallace, G. (1993) (Ed) *Local Management, Central Control: Schools in the Market Place.* Bournemouth: Hyde Publications.

Wang, M.C., Haertel, G.D. and Walberg, H.J. (1990) What Influences Learning? A Content Analysis of Review Literature. *Journal of Educational Research* 84 (1) pp 30-43.

Webb, L. (1967) *Children with Special Needs in the Infants' School.* Smythe: Gerrards Cross.

Wedell, K. (1981) Concepts of Special Educational Need. *Education Today* 31 pp 3-9

Wedell, K. (1988) the New Act: A Special Need for Vigilance. *British Journal of Special Education* 15 (3) pp 98-101.

Wedell, K. (1993) *Special Needs Education: The Next 25 Years.* National Commission on Education. Briefing Paper No. 14. London: NCE.

Weis, T. (1990) Indiana's Prime Time. *Contemporary Education* 62 (1) pp 31-32.

Weiss, C. (1977) *Using Social Research In Public Policy Making.* Lexington, Mass: Lexington Books.

West, A., Hailes, J. and Sammons, P. (1995) Classroom Organisation and Teaching Approaches At Key Stage One: Meeting the Needs of Children with and without Educational Needs in Five Inner City Schools. *Educational Studies* 121 pp 99-117.

Williams, H. and Maloney, S. (1998) Well-Meant, But Failing on Almost All Counts: The Case Against Statementing. *British Journal of Special Education* 25 (1) pp 16-21.

Williamson, O. (1975) *Markets and Hierarchies: Analysis and Antitrust Implications.* New York: The Free Press.

Wise, A.E. (1967) *Rich Schools, Poor Schools.* Chicago: University of Chicago Press.

Wylie, E.C., Morrison, H.G. and Healy, J. (1995) The Progression of Pupils with Special Educational Needs: A Comparison of Standards. *Oxford Review of Education* 21 (3) pp 283-297.

Index